FOCUS
2

# Academic
# Writing
# Skills

**Ranka Curcin**
Humber College

**Mary Koumoulas**
Humber College

**Sonia Fiorucci-Nicholls**
Humber College

Prentice Hall
Toronto, Ontario

**Canadian Cataloguing in Publication Data**

Curcin, Ranka
      Focus 2 : academic writing skills

Includes index.
ISBN 0-13-977588-9

1. English language – Rhetoric.  2. English language – Rhetoric – Problems, exercises, etc.
3. Language arts (Higher). Koumoulas, Mary.  II. Fiorucci-Nicholls, Sonia.  III. Title.
IV. Title: Focus two : academic writing skills.

PE1408.C872 2000        428.6        C99-932200-1

© 2000 Prentice-Hall Canada Inc., Scarborough, Ontario
Pearson Education

Prentice-Hall, Inc., Upper Saddle River, New Jersey
Prentice-Hall International (UK) Limited, London
Prentice-Hall of Australia, Pty. Limited, Sydney
Prentice-Hall Hispanoamericana, S.A., Mexico City
Prentice-Hall of India Private Limited, New Delhi
Prentice-Hall of Japan, Inc., Tokyo
Simon & Schuster Asia Private Limited, Singapore
Editora Prentice-Hall do Brasil, Ltda., Rio de Janeiro

ISBN 0-13-977588-9

Vice President, Editorial Director: Michael Young
Director of Softside Marketing: Tim Collins
ESL Sales Supervisor: Julie Wade
Art Director: Mary Opper
Executive Developmental Editor: Marta Tomins
Production Editor: Matthew Christian
Copy Editor: Karen Rolfe
Production Coordinator: Wendy Moran
Photo Research: Susan Wallace-Cox
Cover and Interior Design: David Cheung
Cover Image: Photodisc
Page Layout: Erich Falkenberg

1 2 3 4 5       04 03 02 01 00

Printed and bound in the United States.

Visit the Prentice Hall Canada Web site! Send us your comments, browse
our catalogues, and more. **www.phcanada.com** Or reach us through e-mail at
**phabinfo_pubcanada@prenhall.com**

# Contents

## Unit 1: The World

### GET READY

### ANALYZE

### LEARN TO WRITE EFFECTIVELY

### WRITE

## EDIT

## EXTEND YOURSELF

## KEEP A JOURNAL

## GO BEYOND THE UNIT THEME

# Unit 2: Sports and Recreation

## GET READY

## ANALYZE

## LEARN TO WRITE EFFECTIVELY

## WRITE

## EDIT

## EXTEND YOURSELF

## KEEP A JOURNAL

## GO BEYOND THE UNIT THEME

# Unit 3: Health and Wellness

## GET READY

## ANALYZE

## LEARN TO WRITE EFFECTIVELY

## WRITE

## EDIT

## EXTEND YOURSELF

## KEEP A JOURNAL

## GO BEYOND THE UNIT THEME

# Unit 4: Adulthood

## GET READY

## ANALYZE

## LEARN TO WRITE EFFECTIVELY

## WRITE

## EDIT

## EXTEND YOURSELF

## KEEP A JOURNAL

## GO BEYOND THE UNIT THEME

# Unit 5: Language and Communication

## GET READY

## ANALYZE

## LEARN TO WRITE EFFECTIVELY

## WRITE

## EDIT

## EXTEND YOURSELF

## KEEP A JOURNAL

## GO BEYOND THE UNIT THEME

# Unit 6: Careers and Professions

## GET READY

## ANALYZE

## LEARN TO WRITE EFFECTIVELY

## WRITE

# Unit 7: Science and Technology

## WRITE

## EDIT

## EXTEND YOURSELF

## KEEP A JOURNAL

## GO BEYOND THE UNIT THEME

# Unit 8: The Media

## GET READY

## ANALYZE

## LEARN TO WRITE EFFECTIVELY

*To our students
and
colleagues*

# Preface

The writing text of this academic series is created for university and college students who need to learn how to write effectively and correctly. It is built around high-interest themes such as the world, science and technology, adulthood, the media, language and communication, sports and recreation, health and wellness, and professions and careers. Sample essays and editing passages reflect different facets of each theme while helping students develop their academic writing skills. Within each unit, there are eight sections.

**Get Ready** is a stage of discovery and probing into already-existing background knowledge about the topic. It gives students an opportunity to generate and exchange ideas and information needed for the writing assignments. This stage allows them to identify the theme-related and appropriate vocabulary essential for convincing and serious academic writing. Through such pre-writing activities as freewriting, group and class brainstorming and discussions, interviews, surveys, questionnaires, and others, students increase their own knowledge, gain self-confidence, and develop a positive attitude toward writing. A good preparation guarantees better results.

The **Analyze** section contains a model paragraph/essay for students to read and analyze. Using a variety of activities, students gain a necessary understanding of the structure, or organization, of the written text. This understanding is achieved through students' direct participation in text analysis both in regard to content, its organization, and the appropriate grammatical structures.

**Learn to Write Effectively** is the teaching section in which students learn how to write clear, correct, and effective paragraphs and essays. Such aspects of effective and correct writing include the learning of paragraph unity, organization and development, topic sentences and supporting statements, introductory and concluding paragraphs, and organizational essay patterns such as example, process, classification, cause and effect, comparison and contrast, and argumentation. Concepts are explained, and students are given an opportunity to practise how to write effectively and correctly.

In the **Write** section, students write their own essays. This is the stage of learning about the subject, shaping information for the reader. It involves the organization and development of ideas. It is the stage of revising—making improvements and corrections—by writing several drafts before a final version is produced.

The **Edit** section helps students practise their editing skills beyond sentence level and improve their knowledge of grammar and sentence structure.

**Extend Yourself** is a research stage needed in a regular academic environment. This section follows up on the theme by providing further research tasks that students can work on outside the classroom setting. Using various research techniques, students gather information and write another essay for additional practice.

**Keep a Journal** provides an opportunity for students to write about the theme from a personal perspective while concentrating on the content rather than grammar. This is a stage to improve students' fluency because it encourages them to generate interesting and relevant content from a personal standpoint.

**Go Beyond the Unit Theme** is the last writing stage. Here, students are encouraged to write on themes other than the unit theme while using the same writing strategies learned in the unit. Motivation and interest are crucial factors in bringing success; having a choice of content may make a world of difference to students and eventually to us as their teachers and readers.

# To the Teacher

The approach to teaching writing in the **Focus 2** academic series is content-based. We believe that motivation plays a crucial role in the learning process. Therefore, the selection of thematic content that appeals to academically bound young adults was the first and most important step in the process of putting this academic writing book together. All sample essays and editing texts are authentic, most of them taken or adapted from university and college textbooks used in regular programs. The reason for the selection from academic sources rather than popular journalistic writing was to familiarize students with the type of content they would be reading and writing about in their own courses. Furthermore, college texts are traditionally written as expository ones and therefore serve as good models of how students should be writing their own assignments.

The level of **Focus 2** is for high intermediate, low advanced students who have already completed an introductory academic course. It is understood that most common and important grammatical structures, as well as paragraph organization and development, have been learned.

**Focus 2** consists of eight units, each divided into eight sections. It is a good idea to teach the units and the sections in the order in which they appear in the book. However, students may skip parts or entire sections of a unit if teachers feel that they do not need any more practice in certain aspects of the writing process. For example, outlining prior to writing their first draft may be an optional activity. Furthermore, teachers may want to teach one writing pattern before another; for instance, cause and effect before comparison and contrast. It is, however, important to check what information has already been presented in earlier units and include it in teaching. Some teachers may not have the time in the classroom to work on all sections in the unit. These units could be assigned as additional or optional work or skipped entirely depending on their students' level. Sections such as **Extend Yourself, Keep a Journal**, or **Go Beyond the Unit Theme** are specifically created for additional writing practice.

Each unit in the book starts with the **Get Ready** section. Through pair, group, and class discussions, students have an opportunity to talk about the topic selected in each unit. At this stage, students' prior knowledge and personal life experience help them generate and share ideas with one another. The exchange of information increases their knowledge about the subject matter and helps them to write more effectively and convincingly.

The sample paragraph/essay not only provides the content that may increase the students' knowledge about the subject matter, but also clearly helps them to recognize the necessary elements of effective writing. In other words, students have plenty of opportunities to analyze how sample paragraphs and essays are organized and developed. Sample paragraphs and essays are written in a style to encourage students to write in a similar way rather than to intimidate them. Only a single writing pattern is presented in each unit so that students can study and practise each strategy before combining them. All units deal with expository writing, and only one pattern dominates in each unit: example, process, cause and effect, comparison and contrast, classification, and argumentation. The essays usually follow a five-paragraph academic essay organization so that students have clear and appropriate models for their essays.

**Learn How to Write Effectively** is the section in which students learn about the writing process, i.e., paragraph organization and development, unity, transition words, thesis statements, parallel structure, essay patterns, introductions, and conclusions. Teachers may want to use this opportunity to focus on individual elements of essay writing as they are presented in each unit and provide students with a set of rules to be applied at a later stage in the writing process.

Further on in each unit, a Grammar Highlights Box indicates which grammatical patterns are essential or most obvious for specific writing patterns. However, since **Focus 2** is not a grammar text, there is not a grammar section. It is left to individual teachers to make decisions how, when, and which grammar to be presented to or reviewed with their students. Again, sample essays may serve as the starting point in analyzing grammatical structures and sentence types.

Students take an active part once more when they start the **Write** section. The first stage is always the brainstorming session, which gives students an opportunity to discuss in groups those issues and concepts they need to write about in their essay. All questions in this section are related thematically to the list of topics that the students choose from. Also, students are strongly encouraged to take notes not only during the group work but also during the class discussion. This information is essential in helping students write.

Another important stage in the writing process is outlining. Asking students to put their ideas in an outline form encourages them right from the start to organize their thoughts clearly and logically. Also, outlining by using a "form" is visual, and students can spot weakness and errors as well as good points more easily. Since the outlining of information is an important study skill, teachers may insist that students produce outlines for their essays before they write their first draft. The outline forms in this book are provided in each unit. However, they are optional. In other words, if teachers find that students have mastered organization and development, they may ask students to skip the outline and write the first draft instead.

It is not always necessary that teachers control all stages of the writing process. Peer checking, when students help one another with the written outline, is therefore suggested. This develops critical thinking and positive criticism skills in students, and, at the same time, it is less threatening because it is coming from a fellow student rather than the teacher.

In each unit, students are asked to produce two drafts and a final version of their essay. The aim of the first draft is to encourage students to concentrate on content and essay organization and development. The purpose of the second draft is to encourage them to edit their work further for appropriate vocabulary and transition words that help unify the paragraph as well as for grammar and mechanics. Any opportunity given to students to go over their work is extremely valuable in the learning process. What the students do not spot the first time, they will spot the second or third.

After the second draft, students still need more feedback from others. Another pair of eyes can see what the writer very often cannot. This should be a very helpful stage if nonjudgmental, not only for weaknesses and errors that need to be worked on and corrected but also in building the students' confidence by encouraging them to share their unfinished work with others. If students are evaluated by their peers in a non-threatening fashion, their confidence and self-esteem undoubtedly increases. In addition, if teachers apply the same criteria when reading and evaluating their students' work, the students will have a much clearer picture of their strengths and weaknesses. As a result, they can concentrate on working on and improving their weaknesses, be that organization or grammar. We all need a "safe" environment to work in. Predictable routines and constant feedback can only contribute to students' progress.

Both students and teachers can use the Peer Evaluation Form when evaluating the students' written work. Teachers will undoubtedly write more detailed comments and observations so that students understand why they have received a certain grade. This form, with the addition of the breakdown in the total grade for each segment, helps teachers stay focused and as objective as possible and, as a result, mark more consistently. The same form/approach may be used in testing situations throughout the course and for final exams so as to provide consistency in marking from the beginning to the end of the course.

The **Edit** section in **Focus 2** is important. Editing is a very difficult skill, which must be practised regularly. We all have a difficult time spotting errors or weaknesses in our own work even after having written and read it several times. Students have an especially hard time correcting their work for grammar and sentence structure. They are able to master the organization and development of paragraph/essay faster and much more easily. However, sentence-level grammar is difficult to master and is the main reason students do not enjoy writing.

Teachers often comment positively on students' content and organization of ideas, but the grade may be a low or failing one despite great ideas. Most often, poor grammar is the reason for our students' poor grades. Students at this level in the language learning process can usually do mechanical grammar exercises successfully. The reason is that there is plenty of time to focus on a particular form and, if students know the grammar rule, are focusing on a particular structure, and are given sufficient time to correct or produce the correct grammar structure, they will be successful. However, when this knowledge about grammar is to be applied in discourse, students lose this ability to monitor for form and accuracy. Therefore, editing practice becomes an essential and crucial point of the writing process. Students gradually improve their observation skills. The more they edit, the better they become in identifying errors and producing grammatically correct sentences. We suggest that editing practice be mostly used as a learning process. Teachers can create their own editing paragraphs based on the class's particular problems. Students should be encouraged to keep the results of all the editing exercises to follow their own progress. There are two editing practice paragraphs in each unit. In some units the number of errors is indicated and the errors are underlined. However, as the students progress through the book, the errors are no longer underlined, but students still know the total number of errors. Finally, in the last two units, there is no indication of the number of errors and students are asked to find them and correct them.

Editing should be done on a regular basis, in class preferably, as well as for homework, and feedback is crucial. Teachers may want to use editing as part of grammar review.

**Extend Yourself** is a stage when students do more in-depth and focused research on their own outside class. The choice of topic may motivate students to do additional "research" and bring their findings to class. The sharing of the written work further helps in building the necessary confidence and in developing those academic skills needed in the students' regular course of study.

Journal writing is an essential part in the writing process. Only by writing on a regular basis, without pressure to produce outstanding and accurate work, can students make progress. Journal writing is a way to express their ideas and feelings more freely simply by the fact that they are not graded on their work. Journal writing can generate a lot of interesting and relevant content as well as provide an occasion to write in a non-threatening atmosphere. This is personal writing, which provides teachers with invaluable information about their students' interests, feelings, views, or attitudes. There are some suggestions as to the list of topics. Teachers can always add to this list to personalize it.

The last section of **Focus 2** provides additional topics not related to the unit theme. This is again optional. Some students may have a difficult time struggling with the theme of the unit. This is an opportunity for them to write about the content that motivates them still using the same writing pattern. Also, this is a section for those students who would like to write more on their own in order to further improve their writing skills.

**Focus 2** units contain about 64 hours of classroom material that could be covered in one term. Since some of the sections in the book are optional, class time can be devoted to grammar lessons and tests. Most of the writing should take place in class. However, some assignments are assigned for homework as part of the preparation for writing. The book offers flexibility to teachers in designing their lessons to suit their students' needs and interests.

# To the Student

Welcome to the **Focus 2** academic series! This is the beginning of an exciting journey of discovering and learning how to write well and effectively. While working through the book, you will have many opportunities to share your knowledge and life experience with other students, as they will with you. Furthermore, you will have a chance to build on your existing knowledge, learn new and effective strategies, and apply all this in your academic writing. The content of the book is presented in a simple and predictable format to make you feel comfortable and in control of your learning process.

The themes such as the world, science and technology, health and wellness, media, adulthood, and others, have been chosen to reflect your interests as a student and young adult. The nature of the content encourages you to participate in a variety of tasks as well as to explore each theme further.

In **Focus 2**, you will be given plenty of opportunities to learn and practise the various styles of academic writing through the writing process approach. This means that you will go through several stages before you write the final version of your essay. You will need to **Get Ready** through pair, group, and class activities, **Analyze** sample essays in terms of content and organization patterns, and **Learn How to Write Effectively** by learning about writing strategies. And, once you are required to **Write**, you will go through the brainstorming, selection, organization, development, and revision stages before you start writing your first draft. At that point, you will edit your work for content and organization and write your second draft. Finally, after peer evaluation, which is additional constructive feedback, and editing for grammar and mechanics, you will be ready to write your final and best version of your assignment. Throughout this entire process your teacher will be there to teach and guide you so that you can produce effective, interesting, and correct essays.

The more you write, the better and more effective writer you will become. Therefore, **Focus 2** gives you an opportunity to **Keep a Journal**, so you can react to issues from a personal point of view, **Extend Yourself** through more in-depth research and preparation for additional writing assignments, and **Go Beyond the Unit Theme** to write about a topic that matters to you, while using the writing strategies and essay patterns learned in your academic English course.

In order to succeed in learning how to write well, effectively, and correctly, it is a good idea to use **Focus 2** systematically so that you can progress steadily. Use the book as a workbook and refer to it and your notes regularly. It is also a good idea to keep a separate file of all your writing assignments and your teacher's comments and suggestions to be able to check on your progress as a writer.

Since you are a student soon to be a professional, it matters how well and correctly you write. It is therefore never too soon to start working on and improving your writing skills. And you can enjoy it even though it is hard work!

# Acknowledgments

The Focus 2 series would not have been written without numerous people who participated in and supported its creation. We are indebted to our colleagues, who encouraged us to undertake such an immense project, and our students, who participated in the testing of the material in this series. Special thanks go to the reviewers of the series, who provided valuable comments and suggestions, including: Jean Black, Brock University; Marilyn Brulart, Douglas College; Patricia Currie, Carleton University; Ellen Davis, George Brown College; Pamela Gifford, Brock University; Lynda Hayward, Douglas College; Sandy McIntosh, University of Alberta; Phyllis Pankratz, Mount Royal College; Kay Sproule, Grant MacEwan College; and Avril Taylor, University of Victoria. We would especially like to thank Marta Tomins, Executive Developmental Editor at Prentice Hall, for her guidance and support, and her genuine interest and enthusiasm for the series. Furthermore, without copyeditor Karen Rolfe's expertise, constructive criticism, support, suggestions, and hard work, Focus 2 would not have been as effective. Equally, Production Editor Matthew Christian's input and excellent organizational skills contributed to a successful completion of the series. We thank everyone at Prentice Hall without whose skills and expertise this series would not have been published. Last, but not least, we would like to thank our families, who supported and encouraged us throughout the project.

# Unit 1

# The World

**After completing this unit, you will be able to**

- analyze a paragraph for unity, organization, and development;

- brainstorm, select, develop, and organize your own paragraph;

- write unified, organized, and well-developed paragraphs;

- write your first, second, and final drafts;

- correct your work using peer checking and revision techniques;

- edit paragraphs for specific grammar and sentence-structure errors.

# GET READY

### Task 1: Let's Talk About the Young in Today's World

Work in a group. Look at the pictures below and answer the following questions.

1. Who do you think people in these pictures are?

2. How are they dressed? What are they wearing?

3. What kind of hairstyles do they have? What do you think is the colour of their hair?

4. What is the girls' make-up like?

5. Where are they? What do you think they are doing?

6. What do you think they are talking about?

7. Look at the way they are dressed and behaving. What do you think their lifestyle is like?

8. What do you think is important to them?

9. How do they view life, the world?

## Task 2: What About You?

On your own, make a list of the following, where applicable:

- clothes you buy/wear (brand names, designer clothes, your own style);
- hairstyle and colour of your hair;
- accessories (earrings, rings) and make-up;
- activities, interests, hobbies you like and have;
- kinds of movies you watch;
- kinds of music you listen to;
- your favourite people (musicians, celebrities, personalities);
- your attitude to at least five issues listed below (jot down some reactions in note form; a list of adjectives to help you respond to this question more effectively is also provided below):

a) education      _____

b) job security _____

c) money      _____

d) relationships   _____

e) family _____

f) politics   _____

g) religion   _____

h) the world      _____

i) the future (yours, the world's) _____

*Some useful adjectives to describe your feelings and opinions:* essential, important, uncertain, strong, crucial, complicated, dangerous, splendid, wonderful, bleak, prosperous, plentiful, different, unpleasant, nuclear, extended, one-parent, doomed, ugly, alarming, fatal, passive, active, starving, deteriorating, tough, exciting, justified, militant, violent, limited, supportive, trustworthy, just, honest, ordinary, overcrowded, wealthy, powerful, destructive, etc.

## Task 3: What Do We Have in Common?

Now work in a group to compare and discuss your answers. How much do you have in common? Do you share the same characteristics? As a group, record this information for each group member so that you can report your findings to the rest of the class.

## Task 4: Let's Share the Information

Share the group's findings with the rest of the class and find out how much your group has in common with other groups. On the blackboard, the teacher will make a list of the common characteristics.

# ANALYZE

## Task 1: Analyzing the Main Idea

The following paragraph discusses some characteristics young people share. First, read the paragraph for general content, answer the questions below, and discuss your answers with the rest of the class.

1. What is the sample paragraph about? Identify the topic sentence.

2. What are the main characteristics young people share? Use a light marker to highlight them.

3. What are some specific examples that the writer uses to illustrate and support the main idea? Underline them.

4. How does the author conclude the paragraph? Is the concluding statement different from the topic sentence? If it is, in what way? Explain.

## Sample Paragraph: Universal Culture

There are many characteristics that young people share today, but the most evident aspect of universal culture is young people's lifestyle. First, one obvious common characteristic is their concern with their appearance. It is extremely important to the young how they look. Therefore, their "obsession" with fashion, that is, what they wear, is natural. Brand name clothing like Nike shoes, designer jeans, Calvin Klein T-shirts, and Adidas jackets make up their wardrobes. They wear crazy and colourful hairstyles. It makes no difference whether we walk the streets of Tokyo, New York, London, or Seoul, young people today look the same. Another characteristic that young people share is that they tend to like similar things. It seems they like the same kind of movies and listen to the same type of music: blockbuster movies like Titanic that have fantastic sound and visual effects; rock bands who are loud and aggressive; and performers who are sleek and stylish. Lastly, the young today seem to think about life quite similarly. They are practical and realistic, as well as quite materialistic. They recognize that their future is unstable, with few guarantees for success and great competition on both personal and professional levels. This means that getting married, having a family, and staying with one person for the rest of their lives is not always the expected reality. Young people tend to choose more practical and better-paying professions such as computer programming, accounting, business management, or engineering. In case of unemployment, these professions give them the flexibility to find another position. Also, they do not expect stability and security for the rest of their lives. It can therefore be concluded that young people today, no matter where they live, tend to have common characteristics with regard to how they live their lives.

## Task 2: Analyzing the Supporting Information and Details

Read the sample paragraph again and complete the chart below.

### Universal Culture

| Appearance | Likes/Interests | Attitudes |
|------------|-----------------|-----------|
| fashion | movies | practical and realistic |
| | | |

## Task 3: Stating an Opinion

Read the sample paragraph one more time and discuss the following questions with your classmates. State your opinions clearly by providing concrete examples to support your views.

1. How do you feel about what you read? Do you find that the paragraph is written in an interesting way or not? What makes you say this?

2. Do you agree or disagree with the writer's views about young people? Why?

3. Are there any aspects of universal culture in regard to young people that the writer did not address? What are some of the aspects that you would write about in your paragraph? Make a list.

# LEARN TO WRITE EFFECTIVELY

In order to write effectively, it is beneficial to master the following aspects of paragraph organization and development.

## The Paragraph

A paragraph contains a group of sentences that develop an idea. The paragraph's main idea is expressed in a topic sentence. It tells you what the paragraph is about. The other sentences of the paragraph provide supporting evidence so that you understand why the writer makes the point that is made. As a writer, you provide supporting information by giving reasons, examples, and details in order to communicate the main idea successfully. The paragraph ends with the concluding statement, which summarizes your main idea. The paragraph stands alone and you can recognize it because the first sentence is indented or there is a double space between it and the preceding paragraph. The length of a paragraph varies from approximately fifty words to three hundred.

## The Topic Sentence

A new paragraph usually begins with a sentence that expresses the main idea. This sentence is called a topic sentence. The topic sentence contains only one main idea, which tells you what the paragraph is about.

## Supporting Sentences

Supporting sentences follow the topic sentence and make up the rest of the paragraph. They provide evidence that the main idea is valid and true. There are many ways to support the main idea. As a writer, you can provide reasons, give examples and explanations, narrate an event, or provide facts. The supporting evidence has to be correct and also sufficiently detailed and specific. Concrete details contribute to the full development of the main idea and help you understand the main idea more easily.

## Paragraph Unity

An effective paragraph has unity or a sense of wholeness. This means that all its sentences relate directly to and develop the topic sentence. When the paragraph has unity, you can read it easily. Any sentence in the paragraph that does not relate to or develop the main idea must be eliminated. Finally, finishing the paragraph with a concluding statement contributes to the sense of wholeness or unity and completion.

## Paragraph Organization

A paragraph has to be organized in such a way so that all sentences are written in a logical order. There are many different ways to organize information in a paragraph but this depends on the topic of the paragraph. For example, if you are providing examples or reasons to support your main idea, you are ordering this information by number, from most to least important support or least to most important support. You can also order the information by time, that is, chronologically, (by telling a story or explaining a process). Yet another way to order information is by space (by describing a place, a person, or a thing). In other words, the ordering of information and the method used depends on the main idea you wish to develop.

---

# The Paragraph

Topic Sentence:

_____

Supporting Sentence (1):

_____

Specific Examples and Details:

_____

Supporting Sentence (2):

_____

Specific Examples and Details:

_____

Supporting Sentence (3):

_____

Specific Examples and Details:

_____

Concluding Sentence:

_____

# Transition Words

When you write a paragraph, it is very important to use transition words, which are the words that connect your ideas. If you do not use transition words, your paragraph will sound "choppy." That means that there is no cohesion in your paragraph. In other words, in order for your paragraph to sound "smooth," use appropriate transition words.

## Typical Transition Words in Paragraphs

These words will help you connect your ideas in the paragraph. The transition words you use depend on the type of the paragraph you write.

**By Number:** first, second, third, another, last, lastly, final, finally, the most important, the best/worst

**By Time:** once, next, second, third, after, as soon as, then, now, while

**By Space:** in front of, above, under, over, around, outside, opposite, behind, below, next to

**By Result:** as a result, therefore, consequently, again, in addition, for example, for instance

**Concluding Statement:** in conclusion, to end, to summarize, in summary, to conclude

## Task 1: Identifying Transition Words

Go back to the sample paragraph and put a box around all the transition words you can find.

## Task 2: Completing the Sample Outline

Now go back to the sample paragraph and read it more carefully to complete the following outline. Compare your finished outline to a partner's outline.

# S a m p l e   O u t l i n e

**Title:** _____

Topic Sentence:

_____

_____

Supporting Sentence (1):

_____

_____

Specific Examples and Details:

_____

_____

Supporting Sentence (2):

_____

_____

Specific Examples and Details:

_____

_____

Supporting Sentence (3):

_____

_____

Specific Examples and Details:

_____

_____

Concluding Statement:

_____

_____

# WRITE

## Brainstorm Together

In a group, discuss the following questions then write down the information in note form and report the findings to the rest of the class. During the class discussion, take additional notes about the information you think is important. This will help you later in writing your own paragraph.

1. What does the term "global village" or "global culture" mean? What do you think brings the world cultures closer together today more than ever before? Give some specific examples.

2. What is the world today like? What are some positive things that you can think of? What are some negative issues that the world faces today? Discuss some specific examples.

3. What are some things that make cultures unique? What is it that makes your culture/country unique? Think of some specific customs, traditions, and celebrations and briefly describe one.

4. How do young people spend their free time? What are some typical things they do? How do you spend your free time? What are your favourite activities and hobbies? What are your interests? Do you think that you do the same things most young people do?

## Choose a Topic

Look at the following list of topics. Select one you would like to write a paragraph about.

1. The world cultures today share many characteristics.

2. Discuss some positive or negative aspects that the world faces today.

3. Describe a special custom or celebration from your country.

4. What do young people do in their spare time?

## Start the Writing Process

Before you start writing the first draft of your paragraph, it is a good idea to go through several preliminary stages. Skipping any of them may result in less effective writing. Those stages are brainstorming, selection, development, organization, peer checking, and revision.

**Brainstorming** is the first stage in the writing process. It is an excellent initial technique to generate ideas on a certain topic. You can do it on your own by simply jotting down any ideas that come to mind without trying to organize them. You can also discuss your ideas in a group or as a class. This exchange of information provides you with a lot of additional information that you either didn't know or didn't think of yourself. The ideas that you generate using this technique include main ideas, supporting ideas, and details and examples.

**Selection** of main ideas, supporting ideas, and details and examples is the second stage in the writing process. This is the time to go over all your notes carefully and choose the most appropriate, interesting, relevant, and convincing ideas that you believe you can develop sufficiently into a paragraph.

**Development** of ideas is the third stage in the writing process. This is the time when you start developing the supporting information and providing details and examples that best illustrate your point of view. If you chose an interesting idea or a detail, but you cannot develop it because you do not have sufficient information, it is much better to drop it and choose another one that you can develop much more easily.

**Organization** of information, or the ordering of information in the form of an outline, is another preliminary stage in the writing process. The outline helps you see the order in which you want your information to appear in the paragraph. As a result, writing a paragraph while referring to your outline ensures that the information is complete and in the order you think is most effective. (There is a sample outline form provided in each unit.)

**Peer checking** is the first and essential step to getting direct feedback from your peers on your outline. Before you start writing your first draft, ensure that your outline contains the necessary information, which is clearly organized, sufficiently developed, and unified. This feedback helps you revise your outline more easily.

**Revision** is the final stage when you go over your partner's comments and suggestions and try to revise or improve your outline in regard to content and its organization and development.

## Task 1: Brainstorming

Now that you've selected your topic, brainstorm as many ideas as possible, including examples. Refer to the notes that you made during the group and class discussions and add to them.

## Task 2: Selection

Go over your notes carefully. Select the main idea and three supporting ideas that you can develop effectively with examples.

## Task 3: Development

Develop the supporting ideas that you have selected. Provide examples and details that best illustrate your point of view.

## Task 4: Organization

Use the outline form provided below to organize the ideas for your paragraph. Refer to the sample outline for assistance.

---

# My Paragraph Outline

### Title: _____

Topic Sentence:

_____

_____

Supporting Sentence (1):

_____

_____

Specific Examples and Details:

_____

_____

_____

Supporting Sentence (2):

_____

_____

Specific Examples and Details:

_____

_____

_____

Supporting Sentence (3):

_____

_____

Specific Examples and Details:

_____

_____

_____

Concluding Statement:

_____

_____

_____

## Task 5: Peer Checking

Show your outline to a partner. Discuss aspects of the outline that are appropriate and make comments and suggestions about those parts that are unclear, incomplete, or inappropriate.

When checking your partner's outline make sure that

1. there is one main idea;

2. there are three supporting ideas;

3. each supporting idea is appropriately developed by using examples and details;

4. there is a general balance to the discussion of each supporting idea.

## Task 6: Revision

Take note of the comments and suggestions made by your partner and use these to revise your outline.

Once you have completed all the preliminary stages to paragraph writing, you are not expected to write your paragraph only once because it is virtually impossible to produce an effective piece of writing in a single effort. You should actually write several versions before you submit your final copy. These versions are called **drafts**. Writing two drafts before your final version should be a minimum to ensure better quality of your written work. Remember that each stage in the writing process is crucial because you cannot focus on everything at once. The more time and effort you put into your work, the more effective your final version will be. Be willing to work with your writing until you are satisfied with it.

# Grammar Highlights Box

The following grammar structures will help you put your ideas together effectively and edit your work.

**Nouns: Count/Non-Count
        Singular/Plural**

There are many *characteristics* that young people share, but it seems that the concern with their *appearance* is especially important.

**Simple Present**

Young people *wear* crazy and colourful hairstyles, and all *have* the same look.

**Subject-Verb Agreement**

*They do not expect* stability and security for the rest of their lives.

**Gerunds and Infinitives**

Young people tend *to choose* more practical and better-paying professions.

**Simple and Compound Sentences**

First, one obvious common characteristic is their concern with appearance.

There are many characteristics that young people share, *but* the most evident aspect of universal culture is young people's lifestyle.

## Task 1: Practising Grammatical Structures

Go back to the sample paragraph and identify other sentences that contain the grammatical structures illustrated in the Grammar Highlights Box.

## Task 2: First Draft

This is the first stage of paragraph writing. You are using the information from your outline (often written in note form) to write a paragraph. In this stage, you should concentrate on the content and the organization and development of your ideas. Use your revised outline to write the first draft of your paragraph.

- Concentrate on the content, organization, and development of your ideas.
- Make sure your topic sentence expresses the main idea clearly and effectively.
- Your concluding sentence must summarize the main idea.

## Task 3: Second Draft

This is the second stage of the writing process. Read your first draft carefully and make necessary changes to make your writing more effective. You should now check for the choice of words, appropriate transitions for paragraph unity, grammar, and mechanics.

Read your draft carefully and check for

- choice of vocabulary
- appropriate transition words
- correct grammar

- punctuation
- spelling

## Task 4: Peer Evaluation

After you have written your second draft, you need some constructive feedback. Peer editing is a very important aspect in the writing process. When you write something, you need someone to read your work and react to it. This reaction is called feedback. You need to know whether your paragraph is good, interesting, clear, appropriate, convincing, well illustrated and correctly written, or poor, boring, confusing, with grammatical errors, incorrectly spelled words, and incorrect punctuation. In other words, peer editing serves as feedback to help you improve your second draft in regard to content, organization, and development of ideas, grammar, and mechanics.

Peer editing should never be judgmental and negative. It should be positive criticism of your writing so that you can improve as a writer. The more positive and relevant feedback you get, the better and more confident a writer you will become.

Work in pairs. Exchange your paragraphs and complete the Peer Evaluation Form.

Look at your partner's comments about your paragraph and make the changes to your paragraph that you think are necessary.

You will find the Peer Evaluation Form in every unit in this textbook. It is designed to help you focus on particular aspects of writing and evaluate them. Since you cannot always easily spot the strong and weak points in your writing, other readers, in this case your peers, can provide invaluable comments by reading your work "critically." Also, bear in mind that teachers apply the same criteria when reading and marking your written work. The Peer Evaluation Form thus shows you how your work is evaluated and graded.

# Peer Evaluation Form

**Writer's Name:**

**Evaluator:**

| | Yes | No | If not, please comment |
|---|---|---|---|
| ORGANIZATION | | | |
| 1. The paragraph contains | | | |
| a clear topic sentence | | | |
| supporting details and examples | | | |
| appropriate transitions | | | |
| concluding sentence | | | |
| CONTENT | | | |
| 1. The choice of ideas is | | | |
| interesting | | | |
| appropriate | | | |
| clearly stated | | | |
| convincing | | | |
| well illustrated | | | |
| GRAMMAR AND MECHANICS | | | |
| 1. Circle or underline any mistakes that you notice in | | | |
| spelling | | | |
| punctuation | | | |
| grammar | | | |

## Task 5: Final Version

The **final version** of your paragraph is a clean copy of your writing that is to be handed in to your teacher to read and correct. As you write, pay attention to all aspects of good writing. Make sure that you have enough time and that you are concentrating on the task so as not to make new errors or miss a line while copying. Make sure that your writing is neat so that it is also visually effective. Always proofread your work before handing it in.

1. Write your final version of the paragraph.

2. Use the Peer Evaluation form to double-check for any weaknesses or errors.

3. Proofread your paragraph before you hand it in.

# EDIT

Editing helps you to improve your grammar and sentence structure beyond the mechanical practice in grammar books. It also helps you to improve your monitoring skills while you write. First, write for ideas and content, then organization, and finally for text that is grammatically correct. Sometimes, it is hard to see your own mistakes. Editing practice helps you to improve your observation skills. The more you edit, the better you become in writing grammatically correct sentences.

Use the following steps when you do editing exercises or edit your own work.

1. Read the text at least once without a pen in your hand so as not to be tempted to start correcting it before you read what the paragraph is about.

2. Once you start correcting the errors, read carefully and look for clues. Certain words indicate whether a tense is incorrect, or the subject does not agree with the verb, or the noun is in the wrong number, or your sentence doesn't sound like a complete thought.

3. Once you correct the whole passage, re-read it a couple of times with corrections to see whether the text "sounds" right to you.

Note: There are two texts for editing practice in each unit. The first editing task is easier because the errors have been identified for you and are underlined. You must determine what type of error it is and correct it. The second editing task, however, is more difficult because you must identify those errors yourself and then correct them.

# Editing 1

There are 18 errors in the following text. Edit for errors in

- word form
- verb tense
- verb form
- wrong word/word choice
- article
- number

When I first came here as <u>a</u> international student, I was truly amazed at the huge <u>numbers</u> of students from different countries. We <u>are</u> all here for a reason, that is, to get a good education. But in the process of <u>learn and gain</u> knowledge in our respective fields of study, we were undoubtedly learning not only about this new culture but also about the <u>cultural</u> of our peers. I soon realized that we were all exposed to a great <u>culture</u> diversity and, without much effort, we <u>changed</u> and adapting to new experiences. Some students tried to maintain certain customs and traditions. For instance, they did not attend classes during certain <u>holiday</u> or celebrations. Others wore traditional clothing and ate <u>his</u> own national foods. However, sooner or later most of us adopted some new customs and attitudes, and we started <u>behave</u> like our English-<u>spoken</u> friends and peers. Gradually, we became more open to new ideas and more <u>flexibility</u> in our acceptance of the new culture.

Today, when I think of <u>these</u> first few months in this new culture, I cannot believe that I <u>am managing</u> to survive here. I know that I have changed a great deal, and now my only concern is how I will fit <u>in</u> my own culture once I graduate and go back home. I am certain that I can see how I have changed, but I know for sure that my family and friends will wonder why I behave <u>strange</u>. To me, going back to my country is both <u>excited</u> and scary, but I am looking forward <u>at</u> the challenge. I believe that I will be able to share my

"new" personality with my countrymen.

# Editing 2

There have been 10 errors introduced into the following paragraph. However, this time they are not underlined. Find them and edit for

- word form
- number
- verb tense
- wrong word/word choice
- verb form

You know, I always thought that my clothes somehow were a statement of

my identify. That is, they make me an individual; they showed the world that I

am unique. Whether I chose long skirt or micro minis, Adidas or Nike, I was

telling the world who I was and what I believed in. I was conservative or a

rebel. The clothes I chosen revealed *my* sense of style. But as I sorted

through the shirts and skirts, I saw how ironic this claim were. Fashion is an

industry. Items used to express my individuality were marketed not only by

runways of Paris but in fashion magazine sold worldwide. My fashion

statements were mass produced and sold by the millions. I bought the image

of myself which someone miles away who had never even heard of my name

had created for me. What I considered novel and dared was in fact domesti-

cated. There were hundreds if not thousands of other woman

walking around wearing exactly the same pair of jeans that I had spent hours

painstakingly choosing. So, where was the individuality in all of these?

From W. Hanna and C. Cockerton, *The Human Project*. (Scarborough, ON, 1998), 111–13, adapted with permission of Prentice Hall.

# EXTEND YOURSELF

**Extend Yourself** is an additional step to further work on improving your writing skills. Now you are required to search for information that is related to the general theme of the unit. There are various ways to obtain this information. For example, you may need to read several newspaper or magazine articles about the topic you are interested in before you can write about it. Or you may want to interview someone who is an authority on the subject, conduct a survey, surf the Internet, read some books, watch television programs, etc., in order to collect sufficient information and become more knowledgeable about the topic you select for your writing assignment. The search, selection, and analysis of this information is what we call research. Therefore, in order to carry out the task successfully, you need to work on it both in and out of class. You will probably need to spend some time in the college or university library, at the computer, or with people who can provide you with necessary information. Always make notes; write down sources such as the authors' names, the book titles, the dates of magazine or newspaper articles, etc. You will need this information to refer to when you write the assignment.

## Task 1: Writing a Comment

Go to the library and look through a couple of daily newspapers and magazines to find an article on one of the topics listed below. Read it carefully and make notes to make sure you understand what the article is about. Then write a one-paragraph (200–250 words) comment to the editor.

- urban explosion
- stereotyping
- discrimination
- fashion/fads
- the Internet
- pollution
- crime/violence
- current political event

## Task 2: Sharing the Story

In groups of four, read your paragraphs to each other. Choose the most interesting and effective paragraph and share it with the rest of the class. Include your group's explanation for selecting it. Then, as a class, vote on the best written paragraph. Discuss why you believe it is the best.

# KEEP A JOURNAL

Start keeping a journal. Record your reactions, views, and feelings about the topic you have been working on in each unit. In this first one, it will be about the world. Concentrate on expressing your ideas and don't think about the correct grammar, vocabulary, or spelling. Your views do not have to be about earth-shattering events. Journal writing helps improve your writing because it encourages you to think about content rather than grammar. However, with regular practice, your grammar and vocabulary will inevitably improve. The teacher may either give you some time in class to write in your journal or ask you to do it as homework. Buy a notebook to write in so that you have all your entries in one place. This helps you monitor your improvement and develop as a writer as well as find ideas when you need them to write other kinds of assignments.

## React to Issues

Choose one of the following to write about:

1. An aspect of your culture that you think is unique.

2. The world in the 21st century. What are your views and feelings? Are you optimistic or pessimistic about the future of the world?

3. Any issue related to the topic **The World**.

# GO BEYOND THE UNIT THEME

## Improve Your Writing Skills Even More

Now you have an opportunity to practise writing about other topics not related to the topic **The World**. However, it is a good idea to use the same writing pattern you have learned in this unit.

Write a paragraph on one of the following topics:

- childhood experiences
- characteristics of a good university or college
- characteristics of a place worth visiting
- a topic of your or your teacher's choice

# Unit 2

# Sports and Recreation

**After completing this unit, you will be able to**

- analyze a paragraph in regard to unity, organization, and development;

- analyze an example essay;

- brainstorm, select, develop, and organize your own essay;

- extend a paragraph into an essay;

- write your first, second, and final drafts;

- write example essays;

- provide appropriate examples to support your arguments.

# GET READY

## Task 1: Let's Make a List

Make a list of all the sports and fitness exercises you can think of. Then highlight the ones that you do yourself or would really like to do if you had enough time or money. Make a new column for those sports that you do not like.

## Freewriting

Freewriting is a way to familiarize yourself with the process of thinking on paper. It is very useful for generating ideas, and as a reference point for future writing tasks. It is a kind of writing that focuses on content and quick reactions to the topic.

Take a piece of paper and write down any idea. Write whatever comes to your mind first. Try not to stop and think too much, especially about how well or correctly you write. This is an exercise that helps you brainstorm ideas based on your personal experience, something you observed, heard, or read about. In other words, you are free to jot down any kind of information that comes to your mind in regard to the topic you are asked to think about. Do not be afraid to write as much as you can—even ideas that seem not directly related to the topic. If you do not know how to continue, keep writing down whatever comes to mind until you are back on track, but do not lift your pen and give up. The more you freewrite, the more ideas you will be able to generate.

## Task 2: Let's Freewrite

Now take 15 minutes and write as much as you can about the sports you really like. Then try to write about the sports and exercises you do not like. Think of some reasons and examples to support your statements.

## Task 3: Let's Talk About Likes and Dislikes

Share your lists with your partner. First, look at the sports you both like and try to explain to each other why you think you like them. Can you recall some situations or give examples that prove to you and your partner that you really like these sports? Use the information from your freewriting exercise. Are there any sports that you both like? Make a list together and state your reasons. You may have the same or different reasons for liking the same sports. Then follow the same procedure for the sports that you do not like.

## Task 4: The Questionnaire: Which Sports Match Your Personality?

Share this information with the rest of the class by listing different sports on the board and discussing why you like them. For example

> *Soccer:* I don't like sports like swimming or yoga that I have to do on my own. I prefer to be with other people and feel a part of a team. I think I like to socialize with others because it's more fun than, for example, running by myself. Another thing is that I like a challenge and I like to win. I think I am competitive. A winning goal makes me feel great.

> *Yoga:* I love it because I can do it on my own without anyone around. I like time to myself without distractions and an opportunity to concentrate. I do not like to take risks, and I stay away from people who are aggressive or competitive. When I exercise, my goal is to be able to concentrate and relax at the same time.

## Task 5: Matching Sports and Students

Look at the figure showing how sports and personality match. Select your favourite sports. Then sit in a group of those students who have chosen the same types of sports as you based on their personality type. Find out why you all chose the same types of sports and what personality characteristics you all share. Finally, present your group's findings to the rest of the class.

---

## Which Sports Match Your Personality?

INSTRUCTIONS: *Fitness experts tell us that if you match your personality with your choice of exercise, the chances are you will stay with your program. Here is a way to do that. Read the description of each psychosocial personality variable, and then rate yourself on the scorecard that follows.*

**Sociability:** Do you prefer doing things on your own or with other people? Do you make friends easily? Do you enjoy parties?

**Spontaneity:** Do you make spur-of-the-moment decisions, or do you plan in great detail? Can you change direction easily, or do you get locked in once you make up your mind?

**Discipline:** Do you have trouble sticking with things you find unpleasant or trying, or do you persist regardless of the obstacles? Do you need a lot of support, or do you just push on alone?

**Aggressiveness:** Do you try to control situations by being forceful? Do you like pitting yourself against obstacles, or do you shy away when you must assert yourself physically or emotionally?

**Competitiveness:** Are you bothered by situations that produce winners and losers? Does your adrenaline flow when you're challenged, or do you back off?

**Mental Focus:** Do you find it easy to concentrate, or do you have a short attention span? Can you be single-minded? How good are you at clearing your mind of distractions?

**Risk-Taking:** Are you generally adventurous, physically and emotionally, or do you prefer to stick to what you know?

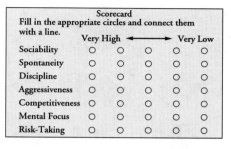

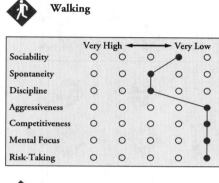

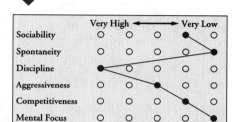

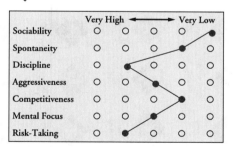

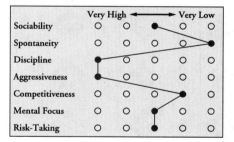

## Understanding Your Score

To see how well your profile matches your sport or exercise activity, look at the four sample profiles in this lab activity. If you have the typical personality of a runner, walker, cyclist, or bodybuilder, your profile should look similar to one of these profiles. If your athletic preference lies elsewhere, turn to the "Your Personality/Your Sport" chart on the next page to see where your acitivities rank on each characteristic. Then compare these rankings with how you scored yourself.

Compared with running, for example, walking is more spontaneous and less aggressive. (It is also safer, in terms of physical stress.) Racquet sports are high in sociability, spontaneity, competitiveness, and focus but low in discipline. Swimming is fairly high in discipline and low in sociability, spontaneity, and aggressiveness.

If you've been having trouble sticking to a fitness program, these charts may help explain why. If you're still looking for a sport, use your findings as a guide.

From *Health and Wellness*, Greenberg and Dintiman (pp. 417–19), "Your Brand of Sweat," by J. Gavin, March 1989, *Psychology Today*, copyright 1989 by Sussex Publishers, Inc. Reprinted with permission from *Psychology Today*.

## Your Personality/Your Sport

Higher ← → Lower

**SOCIABILITY**
Higher: Tennis, Running, Weight Training, Golf, Tennis, Martial Arts, Downhill Skiing, Aerobics, Dance, Weight Training, Cross-Country Skiing
Lower: Walking, Running, Cycling, Yoga, Swimming

**SPONTANEITY**
Higher: Cycling, Swimming, Yoga, Martial Arts, Dance, Aerobics, Walking, Cross-Country Skiing
Lower: Swimming, Yoga, Running, Golf

**DISCIPLINE**
Higher: Tennis, Golf, Downhill Skiing, Weight Training, Martial Arts, Tennis, Aerobics, Walking, Dance, Aerobics, Tennis, Weight Training
Lower: Golf, Downhill Skiing

**AGGRESSIVENESS**
Higher: Martial Arts, Downhill Skiing, Golf, Cycling, Running, Cross-Country Skiing
Lower: Aerobics, Dance, Swimming, Walking

**COMPETITIVENESS**
Higher: Downhill Skiing, Weight Training, Running, Dance, Cycling, Weight Training, Cross-Country Skiing
Lower: Swimming, Aerobics, Walking, Yoga

**MENTAL FOCUS**
Higher: Dance, Yoga, Downhill Skiing, Weight Training, Cycling, Aerobics, Cross-Country Skiing, Swimming
Lower: Running, Walking

**RISK-TAKING**
Higher: Golf, Downhill Skiing, Martial Arts, Tennis, Golf, Cycling, Weight Training, Dance, Cross-country Skiing
Lower: Aerobics, Swimming, Yoga, Running, Walking

# ANALYZE

## Task 1: Analyzing the Main Idea

Read the following paragraph about how we should match sports to our personality. Then answer the questions below with your partner.

## Sample Paragraph: Exercise for Life

Sports and physical exercise are a very important part of our lives. To ensure that we play a sport or exercise regularly, we should try hard to match our personality with the type of sport or exercise that makes us "feel right." First, those of us who are looking for action, a challenge, a competition, are in for a score, and love to play sports with other people should stay away from individual sports no matter how invigorating they might be because the thrill and excitement will probably not be there. Hockey, soccer, basketball, and football are the sports we should practise. On the other hand, those of us looking for relaxation, yet who can easily concentrate, and are not afraid to push on alone, would find it very unfulfilling to join a soccer or a basketball team. Yoga, walking, or running would be perfect sports for us. Finally, if we are adventurous, spontaneous, and spur-of-the-moment types, downhill skiing, martial arts, or tennis would be just right. It is important to be physically active and keep our bodies in shape, but at the same time, we should stick with those sports we can't wait to play or practise again. In other words, if a sport matches our personality we will probably stay active for a long time.

1. What is the main idea of the paragraph? Highlight the topic sentence.

2. How does the writer support his main idea? Underline the supporting statements and number them.

3. If you were to write an essay, which points in this paragraph would you develop? Where would you provide more explanation or give more details and examples? Jot down some suggestions.

## Task 2: Analyzing the Main Ideas and Supporting Information

Now read how the writer has expanded his paragraph into an essay and answer the following questions:

1. What is the essay about? Highlight the main points that the writer discusses.

2. What are the examples that support the writer's statements? List them.

3. Are those examples interesting or not? Why? Are they convincing as a support for the writer's point of view?

4. What kind of examples does he give, and what is their effect on you as a reader?

5. Would you choose similar types of examples for your essay? Why or why not? Explain.

6. Are there any other kinds of examples that could be used to support the main points? What are those?

## Sample Essay: Exercise for Life

The other day I was on my way home when I bumped into a good friend of mine jogging along a busy downtown street. She couldn't stop to chat with me but waved and signaled that she'd call me later. As I continued walking, I suddenly started noticing joggers, cyclists, power walkers, and others involved in physical activities. In a nearby park a group of elderly people were practising tai chi, some youngsters were shooting hoops, and tennis fanatics were waiting for a free court. For the first time in my life I realized that these remarkable events took place every day, but I took them for granted and as part of the usual scene. All those people were doing something they enjoyed, otherwise, they wouldn't be there in this hot, muggy weather. I started thinking about sports and how we all decide to do something, but then some of us stick with it while others stop after a while, blaming it on not having enough time, money, or discipline. Now, the more I think about this, the more convinced I am that the only reason some of us manage to stay with a sport or exercise program is because it "feels right." In other words, being able to match our own personality with the type of sport or exercise will ensure that we stay with it.

First, those of us who are looking for action, a challenge, a competition, are in for a score, and love to play sports with other people should stay away from individual sports no matter how invigorating they might be because the thrill and excitement will not be there. Hockey, soccer, basketball, and football are the sports we should do. I remember when I was just a young kid, our next-door neighbours had three sons who were out in front of their house rain or shine, throwing hoops, kicking a ball, riding bikes in concentrated circles at high speeds, or playing street hockey. In the winter, their father would take them to a nearby skating rink to play hockey three days a week. There were always other children invited to play with the three sons. These sports were perfect for them because they always liked to do everything together and enjoyed competing amongst themselves, winning and fighting when necessary. Therefore, the ability to keep on playing hockey or basketball had to be in their blood. In other words, those of us who are sociable, competitive, and even a bit aggressive should stay away from sports and activities that do not match our personality no matter how invigorating they make us feel. Our personality may well force us to give up on things we do not truly enjoy.

On the other hand, those of us looking for relaxation, but who can easily concentrate, and are not afraid to push on alone would find it unfulfilling to join a soccer or a basketball team. Yet, yoga would be a perfect choice for us. My close friend who's always on the go with a very busy professional life was often down with a cold or the flu. If not sick, she was complaining about having to socialize with people even though she preferred sitting at home with a book or working in the garden. She is an artist and needs to be seen around the city in order to promote her work, but she finds her part-time job at a local library much more relaxing and to her taste. She loves creating her art but hates promoting it. Recently, she joined a yoga class, and she's a changed person. She's much happier, much more relaxed, and claims that she even enjoys meeting people these days. She says that she now practises yoga at home whenever she can and goes regularly to class to improve her style and technique.

She says she discovered a whole new person within her and now realizes for the first time why she couldn't stick to any high-energy, competitive, and aggressive sports and exercises. For people with similar attitudes, yoga or a similar type of sport, such as swimming, might be appropriate.

Finally, for those of us who love adventure and spur-of-the-moment decisions, spontaneity, and a high level of mental concentration, downhill skiing seems to be the right sport. I remember my first encounter with the ski slopes only because of the photos and my parents' stories about our skiing trips together. However, I do remember my first pair of skis quite vividly. Ever since that time I have enjoyed this sport with all my heart. The winter never comes too soon for me—I love it. Now that I'm in university, I don't have as much free time, but I do try hard to take every opportunity to go skiing. I used to train when I was in high school and even compete for a regional team, but eventually I realized that the fun for me was just to ski and not to compete or win. My sense of adventure was always overwhelming as I would go down mountain slopes, brisk wind on my face and sun on my back. Being outside, going down at full speed with the wind pushing me faster was just plain thrilling. Today, I always have the same feelings of anticipation as I head for the mountains. One day, when I get older, I'll probably switch to cross-country skiing, and I know in my heart that I could never settle for swimming, yoga, or soccer.

Sports and physical exercise are a very important part of our lives. They help us stay healthy both physically and mentally. They provide a challenge in our lives. They help us become disciplined, responsible, focused, spontaneous. They help us to become more sociable and tolerant. Most of us are physically able to practise sports and engage in physical activities. Therefore, it is important to recognize which types of sports suit us most so that we can stay with them. It is important to be physically active and keep our bodies in shape, but at the same time, we should stick with the sports we can't wait to play or practise again. Looking forward to Sunday hockey games, yoga classes, or skiing in winter is the greatest thrill of all.

## Task 3: Outlining Information

Read the sample essay once again more carefully and complete the following sample outline.

---

### S a m p l e   O u t l i n e

**Title:** _____

Thesis Statement:

_____

_____

Paragraph 1 Topic Sentence (1):

_____

_____

Paragraph 2 Topic Sentence (2):

_____

_____

Paragraph 3 Topic Sentence (3):

_____

_____

Concluding Statement:

_____

_____

---

## Task 4: Stating an Opinion

Read the sample essay one more time and discuss the following questions with your classmates. State your opinions clearly by providing concrete examples to support your views.

1. How do you feel about what you read? Do you agree or disagree with the writer's views about the matching of a sport or a physical exercise with our personality? Do you think that we can all do any sports if we only set our minds to it? Why or why not?

2. Are there any aspects of matching sports to our personality that the writer did not address? What are some aspects that you would write about in your essay? Make a list.

### Task 5: Comparing Paragraph with Essay Pattern

Compare the sample essay to the paragraph on page 27 and answer the following questions:

1. Which parts of the essay are the same as in the paragraph?

2. Which parts of the essay are new?

3. Where did the writer add them?

4. What kind of information is it? (More details, explanations, examples, etc.?)

5. What do you think is the reason for adding these new parts? What has the writer accomplished in your view?

# LEARN TO WRITE EFFECTIVELY

## The Essay as Extended Paragraph

You already know how to write paragraphs. You know that in a well-written, unified paragraph all sentences relate to each other and develop the main idea, which is the topic sentence. In an organized paragraph, this development is presented in a logical order. The same skills or knowledge are needed to write a well-organized, developed, and unified essay. In other words, an essay is just like a paragraph but expanded.

The main difference between the paragraph and essay is length: an essay is composed of several paragraphs, not just one. It can have a minimum of three paragraphs; an introduction, a middle or body paragraph, and a conclusion. However, many academic essays are longer; most common is a five-paragraph essay. Average essays might be between 250 and 500 words.

The main idea of the entire essay is called the thesis statement. This would be the topic sentence in a paragraph. The thesis statement is then supported by body or support paragraphs. Each of these paragraphs provides support or evidence that the thesis statement is valid. Also, each paragraph has a topic sentence and supporting sentences and details. In other words, the essay may be viewed as an expanded paragraph that provides more detailed support for the main argument.

The following diagram shows how the parts of the paragraph relate to those of the essay:

| Paragraph | Essay |
|---|---|
| Topic Sentence | Introduction and Thesis Statement |
| Supporting statement (1) and details | 1st body paragraph: Topic sentence and supporting statement(s) and details |
| Supporting statement (2) and details | 2nd body paragraph: Topic sentence and supporting statement(s) and details |
| Supporting statement (3) and details | 3rd body paragraph: Topic sentence and supporting statement(s) and details |
| Concluding Statement | Conclusion |

# An Example Essay

The essay you just read is a type of an **example** essay. In an example essay, the reader expects to see concrete, developed examples that help support and clarify the main statement, and strengthen the argument. Besides this, examples make any essay more interesting and enjoyable to read. No matter what topic you are asked to write about, using relevant and carefully selected examples is necessary to develop your paragraphs. Examples clarify or illustrate the main argument you wish to discuss in your essay. Furthermore, they give credibility to your argument or point of view.

Examples are specific references to your personal experiences or someone else's experience(s) that you have witnessed, or heard or read about. They include specific facts, statistics, or information from authoritative sources.

In order to support your main idea, you may wish to use either a series of short, interrelated examples or only one extended example, which illustrates one experience, one person, or one incident that directly relates to and clarifies the main idea. Whichever approach you take, ensure that your examples are carefully selected for relevance since they contribute greatly to the effectiveness of your essay. However, eliminate all those interesting but unrelated examples because they interfere with the unity of your essay and confuse the reader.

## Task 1: Organizing Supporting Ideas and Examples

Read the sample essay again and complete the chart below. Write the main ideas of each paragraph in the three top rows. Fill the three bottom rows with the details for each extended example given.

| Personality and Sports | | |
| --- | --- | --- |
| My neighbour's sons | My artist friend | Myself |
| | | |

## Task 2: Providing Alternative Examples

Now, read each example that the writer provides in his sample essay and write an alternative based on your own experience or from what you observed with other people.

Example 1:

_____

_____

_____

_____

_____

Example 2:

_____

_____

_____

_____

_____

Example 3:

_____

_____

_____

_____

_____

## Typical Transition Words for Example Essays

These words will help you to connect your ideas by linking examples to supporting statements and the main idea and adding coherence to your essay.

| | |
|---|---|
| for example | such as |
| for instance | thus |
| to illustrate | in particular |
| to clarify | suppose, let's suppose |
| take the case of | in fact |
| like | indeed |

## Task 3: Identifying Transition Words

Go back to the sample essay and circle all the transition words you can find.

## Task 4: Completing the Sample Outline

Go back to the sample essay one more time and complete the following outline. Compare your finished outline to your partner's outline.

---

# S a m p l e   O u t l i n e

### Title: _____

Thesis Statement:

_____

A. Paragraph 1 Topic Sentence:

_____

_____

Supporting Statements and Example(s):

_____

_____

B. Paragraph 2 Topic Sentence:

_____

_____

Supporting Statements and Example(s):

_____

_____

C. Paragraph 3 Topic Sentence:

_____

_____

Supporting Statements and Example(s):

_____

_____

Concluding Statement:

_____

_____

# WRITE

## Brainstorm Together

### Task 1: Exchanging Information

In groups of four, discuss the following questions. Think of some specific examples that you recall from your own or somebody else's experience and exchange this information with other members of the group. Take extensive notes, which will help you to write your own essay later.

1. Which team sports do you think of as potentially aggressive? Why? Make a list of these sports as well as the reasons. Think of some incidents that you or others witnessed, or that you have read or heard about.

2. Which famous athletes can you think of? What sports do they participate in? What kind of people do you think they are? Do you believe that any of us could achieve the same results if we set our minds to it? What makes them special? Do you know any sports incidents that involve a famous athlete? How would you rate this athlete as a person? Highly respected, somewhat respected, or not respected. Why?

3. Have you ever been a member of a fitness or sports club? What kind? Describe it briefly. Why did you join? Can we stay in shape on our own, or do we need the kind of discipline provided by such places? What examples and facts can you provide to prove that fitness clubs are a good way to stay in shape and be healthy?

4. Have you ever tried any risk-taking, adventurous sports? Which ones can you think of? Why do you think they may be potentially dangerous, even life-threatening? Think of some stories or even tragedies that you witnessed, heard, or read about to prove how dangerous some of these sports are.

## Choose a Topic

### Task 2: Adding to Notes

Go over your notes carefully and decide which of the following topics you would enjoy writing about. Once you have selected your topic, you may add a few more questions that may be important to you, and which haven't been discussed before.

Your teacher will ask you to develop a three, four, or five-paragraph essay (an introductory thesis statement, the body paragraph(s), and a concluding statement).

1. Competitive team sports are potentially aggressive.

2. Professional athletes are very competitive people.

3. Joining a fitness centre is a good way to stay in shape and be healthy.

4. Some risk-taking sports such as cliffhanging, car racing, and downhill skiing are potentially dangerous.

## Task 3: Talking About the Same Topic

Now sit with another person or a group of students who selected the same topic. Exchange information and discuss the additional questions. Make sure to add to your original notes.

# Start the Writing Process

**Brainstorming**. You have completed this phase in group work. Just add anything else that comes to mind at this point.

**Selection**. Go over your notes very carefully and select one, two, or three main ideas that you can develop effectively with examples.

**Development**. Develop the ideas that you have selected. Provide either one extended example for each main idea (see the sample essay) or two to three short interrelated examples that best illustrate your point of view.

**Organization**. Use the outline form provided to organize the ideas for your essay. Refer to the sample outline for help.

---

## My Example Essay

Title: _____

Thesis Statement:

_____

A. Paragraph 1 Topic Sentence:

_____

_____

Supporting Statements and Example(s):

_____

_____

B. Paragraph 2 Topic Sentence:

_____

_____

Supporting Statements and Example(s):

_____

_____

C. Paragraph 3 Topic Sentence:

_____

_____

Supporting Statements and Example(s):

_____

_____

Concluding Statement:

_____

**Peer Checking**. In pairs, show your outlines to each other. Discuss aspects of the outline that are appropriate and make comments and suggestions about those parts that are unclear, incomplete, or inappropriate.

When evaluating your partner's outline, make sure that

- there are one, two, or three main ideas;
- each main idea is appropriately developed and clearly supported by an example(s);
- there is a general balance to the discussion of each idea if you have more than one.

**Revision**. Take note of the comments and suggestions made by your partner and use them to revise your outline.

# Grammar Highlights Box

The following grammar structures will help you put your ideas together effectively and edit your work.

**Simple Present**

For those of us who *love* adventure, downhill skiing *seems* to be the right sport.

One day when I *get* older, I will probably switch to cross-country skiing.

She *says* that she now *practises* yoga at home and *goes* regularly to class.

**Present Continuous**

Those of us who *are looking for* action and competition should stay away from individual sports.

**Simple Past**

The other day I *was* on my way home when I *bumped* into a good friend of mine jogging along a busy downtown street.

In the winter, the father *would take* them to a nearby skating rink.

**Past Continuous**

All those people *were doing* something they enjoyed.

If not sick, she *was complaining* about having to socialize with people.

**Gerunds and Infinitives**

I started *thinking* about sports and how we all decide *to do* something.

As I continued *walking*, I suddenly started *noticing* joggers, cyclists, and others involved in physical activities.

**Modals**

She *couldn't* stop to chat with me but waved and signaled that she *would* call me later.

We *should* stay away from individual sports.

My personality *may* well force me to give up on things I do not truly enjoy.

> **Adjectives/Comparatives**
>
> She is much *happier*, *more relaxed*, and claims that she even enjoys meeting people these days.
>
> Being outside, going down at full speed with the wind pushing me *faster*, was just plain thrilling.

## Task 4: Practising Grammatical Structures

Go back to the sample essay and identify other sentences that contain the grammatical structures illustrated in the Grammar Highlights Box.

## Task 5: First Draft

Use your revised outline to write the first draft of your essay.

1. Concentrate on the content and organization and development of ideas.

2. Have a thesis statement and a concluding sentence.

## Task 6: Second Draft

Read your draft carefully and check for

- choice of vocabulary
- appropriate transition words
- correct grammar
- punctuation
- spelling

## Task 7: Peer Evaluation

Work in pairs. Exchange your essays and complete the Peer Evaluation Form. Then look at your partner's comments about your essay and make the changes to your essay that you think are necessary.

# Peer Evaluation Form

**Writer's Name:**

**Evaluator:**

| | Yes | No | If not, please comment |
|---|---|---|---|
| ORGANIZATION | | | |
| 1. The thesis statement | | | |
| is clear | | | |
| includes three parallel ideas | | | |
| 2. Each paragraph contains | | | |
| a clear topic sentence | | | |
| supporting detail and examples | | | |
| appropriate transitions | | | |
| 3. The conclusion summarizes the main idea of the essay. | | | |
| CONTENT | | | |
| 1. The choice of ideas is | | | |
| interesting | | | |
| appropriate | | | |
| clearly stated | | | |
| convincing | | | |
| well illustrated | | | |

| | Yes | No | If not, please comment |
|---|---|---|---|
| GRAMMAR AND MECHANICS | | | |
| 1. Circle or underline any mistakes that you notice in | | | |
| spelling | | | |
| punctuation | | | |
| grammar | | | |

## Task 8: Final Version

1. Write the final version of your essay.

2. Review the completed form from Task 4 to double-check your work for weaknesses or errors.

3. Proofread your essay before you hand it in.

# EDIT

## Editing 1

There are 11 errors in the following text. Edit it for errors in

- subject/verb agreement
- verb tense
- word choice/wrong word
- number
- word form

For many of us it is difficult to understand what makes college and university house leagues so competitive and aggressive. What <u>make</u> those students who are normally sane, responsible, and reasonable become so hateful, bitter, and hostile towards one another all in the name of being the "winner"?

The other Sunday, my <u>classmates</u> who loves to go to all sorts of college sports events invited several of us to the final hockey game of the season. The arena was packed. The teams <u>step</u> on the ice, and the game started smoothly. The crowd began cheering on the players, <u>shout</u> out their names and encouraging them to go faster, hit the puck, and get it <u>in</u> the net. Unexpectedly, the first goal was scored and everyone went wild. From that moment on, the game became rougher and the players started pushing and <u>shove</u> one another. Then, after a short while, the referee made some "questionable" decision and was instantaneously confronted with an obscenity-shouting <u>teams</u>. After a long argument, the call stood and the game continued, but hostilities and "hatred" <u>run</u> high and, from that moment, the game held no enjoyment for me.

I cannot understand why people who are in other circumstances quite kind and pleasant, <u>overreacts</u> so outrageously. It seems that this kind of macho, trash-talking, and must-win-at-any-cost behaviour is encouraged in our teams, and <u>spectator</u> contribute a great deal to it by behaving outrageously themselves.

After this "very enjoyable and pleasant" sports event, I decided not to attend any of the house league games again since there <u>is</u> complete disregard for fair play.

# Editing 2

There have been 10 errors introduced into the following paragraph. Find them and edit the text for errors in

- word form
- number
- subject/verb agreement

For years medical experts, especially health psychologist, have promoted regular exercise. Yet only a fraction of the general populations is highly active, and as much as 70 percent of the entire population can be characterized as inactive. Many studies shows that regular aerobic exercise contributes greatly to our physical and mental fitness. Aerobic exercise such as running, swimming, brisk walk, bicycling, rowing, and jumping rope is exercise that uses the large muscle groups in continuous, repetitive action and require increased oxygen intake and increased breathing and heart rates. Aerobic exercise should be performed regularly, three or four time a week for 20 to 30 minutes, with additional five- to ten-minute warm-up and cool-down periods.

The importance of regular, systematic aerobic exercise in keeping the cardio-vascular system healthy cannot be overemphasized. This is true for people of all age. Even preschoolers receive cardiovascular benefits from planned exercise. At the other end of the age spectrum, regular, plan exercise greatly helps older people to strengthen their muscles and bones. Strenuous workouts would not transform an 87-year-old man into Arnold Schwarzenegger, but significant increases in muscle strength have been recorded even in people pushing 100.

We do not need to become marathon runner or spend several hours a day sweating and grunt in a fitness centre to enjoy maximum benefits of exercise. Even a daily brisk walk of 30 minutes or more helps us to stay healthy and live longer.

From E.R. Wood et al, *The World of Psychology* (Scarborough, ON, 1998), 392, adapted with permission of Prentice Hall Allyn and Bacon Canada.

# EXTEND YOURSELF

## Task 1: Interviewing

Interview a college or university athlete, coach, sports fan, or a college or university paper sports writer. Check some sports magazines for interviews to help you prepare a list of 7–10 questions. During the interview, take extensive notes. You will need this information to write about the person and the sport.

Some possible questions for an athlete are the following:

1. When did you first start training? Do you remember the first time you played competitively? Tell me about it.

2. Why did you choose to play (hockey, soccer)? Practise (swimming, running)?

3. What do you think about yourself as an athlete? Is it more important for you to compete or to win? Why?

4. How do you feel about an opposing team or another athlete when you are in competition?

Some possible questions for a sports fan:

1. Do you watch any sport, or do you have favourite sports that you never miss? What are those sports or athletic events?

2. What do you do when your team or athlete is winning or losing? How do you cheer them on? Tell me about a sports event that you remember vividly.

3. Why do you think you watch and follow sports events?

4. Are you involved in any sports or physical activity yourself? Which one(s)? How regularly do you practise sports or exercise?

## Task 2: Reporting

Write an essay about a person you interviewed. Include a personal story, experience, or incident that the person shared. Use it as an extended example to illustrate the main point in your essay.

## Task 3: Sharing the Story

Read your essay in groups of three. As a group, discuss your reactions to each other's work. Then report the discussion to the rest of the class.

# KEEP A JOURNAL

## React to Issues

Choose one of the following to write about:

1. Your favourite sports or exercise.

2. A sports-related story.

3. Your favourite athlete.

4. Any issue related to the topic **Sports and Recreation**.

# GO BEYOND THE UNIT THEME

## Improve Your Writing Skills Even More

Now you have an opportunity to practise writing about other topics not related to the topic **Sports and Recreation**. However, it is a good idea to use the example essay pattern you have learned in this unit.

Write an example essay on one of the following topics:

- characteristics of a movie genre (comedy, drama, horror, science fiction, etc.)
- healthy eating habits
- characteristics of good parents
- a topic of your or your teacher's choice

# Unit 3

# Health and Wellness

**After completing this unit you will be able to**

- analyze an example essay;
- write example essays;
- write well-constructed thesis statements.

# GET READY

## Task 1: What Is the Perfect Life?

Look at the following list. Pick 10 factors that you think are important to you in having a perfect life. After you have selected the 10 factors, rank them in order of importance. Number 1 is the most important and number 10 is the least important. You may add a few of your own factors.

_____ driving an expensive car

_____ being an excellent student

_____ being popular

_____ being self-confident

_____ being able to say "no" without feeling guilty

_____ being physically attractive

_____ enjoying outdoor activities

_____ being the ideal weight

_____ maintaining a regular exercise program

_____ being respected by people

_____ having a good sense of humour

_____ having a general feeling of happiness and satisfaction

_____ having the "perfect" body

_____ being well organized and competent in work habits

_____ being able to manage stressful situations

_____ being in love

_____ being financially secure

_____ other _____

_____ other _____

_____ other _____

## Task 2: Categorize Information

Look carefully at the factors you have selected. Categorize them according to physical, emotional, or mental health.

> Note: Some might fit into more than one category.

| Physical Health | Emotional Health | Mental Health |
|---|---|---|
|  |  |  |

## Task 3: Let's Compare Our Choices

In groups, compare your selections and discuss your choices.

## Task 4: Let's Survey the Class

Walk around the class and find the 10 most popular choices. How many of the class choices were the same as yours? Report this information back to the rest of the class.

# ANALYZE

## Task 1: Analyzing the Main Ideas and Supporting Information

The following essay discusses aspects of health and gives examples of each aspect. Read the essay and react to its content.

- What are the main issues the writer addresses in the essay? Highlight them.
- How does he support his arguments? Look for some examples and underline them.

## Sample Essay: The Meaning of Health

When people are asked to list the most important factors in their

lives, the answers vary widely. Some might say love, financial stability, happiness, a big house, and a bright future. It seems that many people take health for granted. Even if they include health as one of their answers, they usually refer to physical health. Unfortunately, that is not enough. One can be physically healthy, but at the same time lonely, unhappy, or under stress. Being healthy means being physically, emotionally, and mentally healthy.

First and foremost, people are physically healthy if they are physically fit. In other words, they are able to carry out daily duties, can endure physical strain, have lots of energy and get through the day without getting too tired. Healthy people also exercise on a regular basis, sleep well and sufficiently, and eat well but maintain a desirable weight. In other words, exercising three to four times a week, sleeping an average of eight hours, and eating three meals a day with lots of fruits and vegetables contributes to people's good physical health. Also, healthy people do not suffer from diseases and, if they get a cold or the flu, they recover quickly.

However, being only physically healthy is not enough. In order to be healthy, people must also be emotionally healthy. This means that they are happy with their lives and themselves. They are able to cope or deal with stressful situations and can control their anger. They do not run away from problems—they face them and try to solve them. These people also know how to relax and laugh about things that happen to them. Also, when they need help, they seek it from the ones they love and trust. If people didn't recognize the importance of emotional health as part of their whole well-being, they would probably eventually get sick.

Finally, mental or intellectual health is as important as the other two aspects of health. If, after making a mistake, people keep repeating it and do not learn anything from the experience, they are bound to react emotionally, which can trigger physical problems. Since people face stressful situations in both their professional and personal lives, it is essential to learn how to handle problems, and that mistakes are part of daily life. If people continue to make wrong decisions or put themselves and others in dangerous situations or allow their emotions to dictate and control their decisions, the consequences could be unpleasant— even outright devastating. Therefore, it is crucial to understand and analyze the problems and situations people find themselves in so as to avoid emotional conflicts, which may have a direct effect on people's mental health.

In conclusion, being and staying healthy is not an easy task. People are responsible for their own well-being. In order to have a better quality of life and live longer, people need to recognize that not only the "perfect body"—but also their emotional and mental states—are essential.

## Task 2: Organizing Supporting Information

Read the essay again and complete the chart below.

1. State the other two aspects of health discussed in the essay.

2. List additional supporting information about each aspect of health.

|  | Health | |
|---|---|---|
|  | **Emotional** |  |
| regular exercise | deal/cope with stressful situations | problem-solving |
|  |  |  |

## Task 3: Stating an Opinion

1. How do you feel about what you read? Do you agree or disagree with the writer? Why?

2. Are there any aspects of health that the writer did not address?

3. What are some examples that you would like to add to the above chart?

# LEARN TO WRITE EFFECTIVELY

## The Thesis Statement

The essay you just read is a sample of the example essay you learned about in Unit 2. As with any essay, the thesis statement is crucial to the organization and development. In simple terms, what a topic sentence is to a paragraph, a thesis statement is to an essay.

A topic sentence introduces the main idea in a paragraph; the thesis statement states the main ideas of an essay. Each idea stated in the thesis statement becomes the topic sentence of each body paragraph in the essay.

---

### The Meaning of Health

Thesis Statement:

Being healthy means being physically, emotionally, and mentally healthy.

Paragraph 1 Topic Sentence:

First and foremost, people are physically healthy if they are physically fit.

Paragraph 2 Topic Sentence:

In order to be healthy, people must also be emotionally healthy.

Paragraph 3 Topic Sentence:

Finally, mental or intellectual health is as important as the other two

aspects of health.

---

## Parallel Structure in a Thesis Statement

When writing a thesis statement, certain grammatical rules of parallelism must be followed. Parallelism means that the main ideas of the thesis statement are expressed through parallel (or the same) grammatical structures.

Example: Being healthy means being *physically*, *emotionally*, and *mentally* healthy.

"Physically," "emotionally" and "mentally" belong to the same grammatical category of adverbs. This is an example of adverb parallel structure.

This is not the only way to express the main idea of the thesis statement. Other grammatical forms such as nouns, gerunds, infinitives, phrases and clauses, tenses, etc. can be used. The key is to maintain a consistent structure.

Some other ways to express this thesis statement could be as follows:

**Adjective Parallel Structure**: Being healthy includes *physical, emotional,* and *mental* well-being.

**Gerund Parallel Structure**: Being healthy means *participating* in physical activities, *having* emotional stability, and *stimulating* mental development.

**Clause Parallel Structure**: Being healthy means *that we take care of our physical, emotional, and mental well-being.*

## Task 1: Writing Thesis Statements

The main ideas listed below are in note form. Write a thesis statement for each using the information you are given. Remember to use parallel structure. First look at the following example:

Physical Health
- regular exercise
- balanced diet
- healthy lifestyle

Thesis statement: To maintain physical health, one should exercise regularly, eat a balanced diet, and lead a healthy lifestyle.

Dealing with Stress
- exercise
- time management
- social activities

Thesis statement:_____

_____

Emotional Health
- self-confidence
- effective coping strategies
- positive thinking

Thesis statement:_____

_____

Social Health
- ability to interact with people and environment
- interpersonal relationships
- ability to adapt to various situations

Thesis statement:_____

_____

Spiritual Health
- belief in a unifying force
- connections to other humans
- a purpose to life

Thesis statement:_____

_____

Environmental Health
- appreciation of external environment
- protection of the environment
- improving environmental conditions

Thesis statement:_____

_____

## Task 2: Completing the Sample Outline

Go back to the sample essay and read it more carefully to complete the following outline. Compare your finished outline to a partner's outline.

---

# S a m p l e   O u t l i n e

### Title: _____

Introduction: When people are asked to list the most important factors in their lives, the answers vary widely. Some might say love, financial stability, happiness, a big house, and a bright future. Others might say health. It seems that many people take health for granted. Even if they include health as one of their answers, they usually refer to physical health. Unfortunately, that is not enough. One can be physically healthy, but at the same time lonely, unhappy, or under stress.

Thesis Statement:

_____

A. Paragraph 1 Topic Sentence:

_____

_____

Supporting Details:

_____

_____

B. Paragraph 2 Topic Sentence:

_____

_____

Supporting Details:

_____

_____

C. Paragraph 3 Topic Sentence:

_____

_____

Supporting Details:

_____

_____

Conclusion:

In order to have a better quality of life and live longer, people need to recognize

that not only the "perfect body"—but also their emotional and mental states

are essential.

# WRITE

## Brainstorm Together

Interview a classmate. Ask the following questions and record the information. Report the findings to the rest of the class.

1. Do you have any bad habits? We can be addicted to some (e.g., smoking, excessive drinking, eating junk food, etc.) Are you addicted to any? Which one(s)? How long have you been addicted? Do you remember when and how you started it? Why did you start it? How is this habit affecting you? Give some examples. Do you want or plan to quit the habit? If the answer is "Yes," how are you going to do it?

2. What do you think "stress" or "stressed out" means? Are you ever stressed out? How do you know that you are under stress? What are the

symptoms? When you are "stressed out," what do you do? Give specific examples.

3. What do you do in your spare time to relax? Are you active? What kinds of things do you do when you are by yourself or with friends? What are your favourite activities? Give examples.

# Choose a Topic

Look at the following list of topics. Select one you would like to write about.

1. What are some bad lifestyle habits that can affect our health?

2. What are some ways of dealing with stress?

3. What are some ways to relax?

# Start the Writing Process

**Brainstorming.** Now that you've selected your topic, brainstorm as many ideas as possible, including examples.

**Selection**. Go over your notes very carefully. Make sure that you select three main ideas that you can develop effectively with examples.

**Development**. Develop the ideas that you have selected. Provide examples with supporting statements and details that best illustrate your point of view.

**Organization**. Use the example outline form provided to organize the ideas for your essay. Refer to the sample outline to help you.

## My Example Outline

Title: _____

Introduction/Hook:

_____

Thesis Statement:

_____

Idea 1:

_____

Idea 2:

_____

Idea 3:

_____

A. Paragraph 1 Topic Sentence:

_____

_____

Supporting Examples and Details:

_____

_____

B. Paragraph 2 Topic Sentence:

_____

_____

Supporting Examples and Details:

_____

_____

C. Paragraph 3 Topic Sentence:

_____

_____

Supporting Examples and Details:

_____

_____

Conclusion:

_____

_____

**Peer Checking.** In pairs, show your outlines to each other. Discuss aspects of the outline that are appropriate and make comments about those parts that are unclear, incomplete, or inappropriate.

When evaluating your partner's outline, make sure that

- there are three main ideas;
- each main idea is appropriately developed and clearly supported by examples;
- there is a general balance to the discussion of each main idea.

**Revision.** Take note of the comments and suggestions made by your partner and use these to revise your outline.

# Grammar Highlights Box

The following grammar structures will help you put your ideas together effectively and edit your work.

**Simple Present**

It *seems* that people *take* health for granted.

They also *exercise* on a regular basis, *sleep* well and sufficiently, and *eat* well but *maintain* a desirable weight.

**Modals**

Some people *might* say love, financial stability, happiness, a big house, and a bright future. Some *might* say health.

One *can* be physically healthy, but at the same time lonely, unhappy, or under stress.

In order to be healthy, people *must* also be emotionally healthy.

**Gerunds**

If after *making* a mistake people keep *repeating* it, they are bound to react emotionally.

**Infinitives**

They are able *to carry out* daily duties, they are able *to cope* or *deal* with stressful situations.

They face problems and try *to solve* them.

**First and Second Conditional**

People are physically healthy *if they are physically fit*.

*If people didn't see the importance of emotional health as part of their whole well-being,* they would probably eventually get sick.

## Task 1: Practising Grammatical Structures

Go back to the sample essay and identify other sentences that contain the grammatical structures illustrated in the Grammar Highlights Box.

## Task 2: First Draft

Use your revised outline to write the first draft of your essay.

- Concentrate on the content, organization, and development of your ideas.
- Make sure your introduction includes an interesting hook and a parallel thesis statement.
- Your conclusion must summarize your major points.

## Task 3: Second Draft

Read your draft carefully and check for

- choice of vocabulary
- appropriate transition words
- correct grammar
- punctuation
- spelling

## Task 4: Peer Evaluation

Work in pairs. Exchange your essays and complete the Peer Evaluation Form. Then look at your partner's comments about your essay and make the changes to your essay that you think are necessary. You might have to further edit your essay.

---

# Peer Evaluation Form

**Writer's Name:**

**Evaluator:**

|  | Yes | No | If not, please comment |
|---|---|---|---|
| ORGANIZATION | | | |
| 1. The introduction grabs my attention. | | | |
| 2. The thesis statement | | | |
| is clear | | | |
| includes three parallel ideas | | | |

| | Yes | No | If not, please comment |
|---|---|---|---|
| 3. Each paragraph contains | | | |
| a clear topic sentence | | | |
| supporting details | | | |
| appropriate transitions | | | |
| CONTENT | | | |
| 1. The choice of ideas is | | | |
| interesting | | | |
| appropriate | | | |
| clearly stated | | | |
| convincing | | | |
| well illustrated | | | |
| GRAMMAR AND MECHANICS | | | |
| 1. Circle or underline any mistakes that you notice in | | | |
| spelling | | | |
| punctuation | | | |
| grammar | | | |

## Task 5: Final Version

1. Write the final version of your essay.

2. Use the Peer Evaluation Form to double-check your work for weaknesses or errors.

3. Proofread your essay before you hand it in.

# EDIT

## Editing 1

There have been 12 errors introduced into the following text. Edit for errors in

- word form
- number
- wrong word/word choice
- verb tense
- sentence structure
- parallel structure

To manage stress, you need to set aside time. To exercise regularly and <u>engaging</u> in other health-promoting activities, you also need to set aside time. Since stress can capture your attention, energy, and time. <u>It</u> can interfere with your wellness regimen. After all, stress can be a threat to your physical self or to your self-concept. Who can blame you for <u>to postpone</u> or <u>to cancel</u> wellness activities such as exercise to manage that threat? This section shows you how to organize your time better so you have plenty of <u>times</u> for exercise, <u>manage</u> stress, and the myriad of other wellness activities you need, and choose, to do.

To be serious about using time-management strategies you need to realize that:

1. Time is one of your most precious <u>possession</u>.

2. Time spent is gone forever.

3. You cannot save time. Time moves continually and it is used, one way or another. If you waste time there is no bank where you can withdraw the time you previously saved to replace the time wasted.

4. To come to terms with your mortality is to realize that your time is limited. None of us will live forever, and none of us will be able to do <u>anything</u> we would like to do.

You can invest time to free up (not to save) more time than you originally <u>invest</u>. Then you will have <u>sufficiently</u> time to use stress management techniques such as <u>to assess</u> how you spend time, prioritizing and freeing up time for wellness. The bottom line of time management is that you need to invest time initially in order to free it up later.

From J.S. Greenberg and G.B. Dintiman, *Wellness* (Needham Heights, MA 1997), pp. 70, 71, 77, adapted by permission of Allyn & Bacon.

# Editing 2

There are 14 errors in the following text. Edit it for errors in

- verb tense
- wrong word
- verb form
- number
- word form
- subject-verb agreement

It is a well-known fact that smoke is a bad and danger habit. I remember when I was young, my father use to smoke and my mother always complained about it. The minute he would wake up, he would have his cigarette. There was no doubt that smoking is addictive. Research show that there is a direct link between smoking and various lung and heart disease. At one point my father tried to stop smoking but he ended up being quite sick with a fever and wouldn't go to working. It looked like to quit was out of the question since he was always in a bad mood and not very pleasant to the family. I remember to watch him struggle, and I promised myself I would never smoke. A few year later, however, I did pick up this bad habit while I was in high school. My friends would say, "Come on, man. It's cool." Anyway, everyone were doing it and I didn't want to be left out. However, as soon as I got involved in sport, I realized that smoking didn't help much. I had problems breathing and I couldn't endure the training like the other guys who aren't smokers. Quitting wasn't easy but I am succeeded, and now I know I did the right thing.

# EXTEND YOURSELF

## Option 1

### Task 1: Looking Through Periodicals

Go to the library and find two or three newspaper or magazine articles about a particular bad health habit (e.g., smoking, alcoholism, eating disorders, drug use, etc.). Read them carefully and make notes of the main issues that interest you. Then add specific examples that seem particularly interesting and that you haven't heard or read about before.

### Task 2: Writing About Bad Habits

Use the notes you've made and write an essay describing the habit you selected and steps for treating it.

## Option 2

### Task 1: Creating a Questionnaire

Go to the library and browse through various magazines that have health and wellness questionnaires similar to the example below. Copy this information and bring it to class.

    In a group, share the collected questionnaires and develop your own health and wellness assessment questionnaire. Make sure that the questionnaire includes explanations of any aspect of health you are addressing. A sample questionnaire is provided below.

## The Questionnaire: How Healthy Are You?

Answer "Yes" or "No" to the following questions about your general state of health.

    Depending on your answers you will know how healthy you are.

1. Are you a very happy person?

2. Do you eat regularly? Three meals a day?

3. Are you often sick?

4. Do you go for a regular medical checkup?

5. Do you exercise three times a week?

6. Do you sleep between 7 to 8 hours each night?

7. Are you often stressed out?

8. Do you get angry easily?

9. Do you socialize with friends regularly?

10. Do you have people to talk to about your problems?

11. Do you always help others?

12. Do you regularly spend time alone?

If you answered "Yes" to questions 1, 2, 4, 5, 6, 9, 10, 11, and 12, and "No" to questions 3, 7, and 8, you are probably quite healthy.

## Task 2: Interviewing

Ask someone (e.g., a classmate, a relative, or a friend, etc.) to complete the questionnaire that you created in your group. Collect it and use it as a source of information to write an essay describing the person's general state of health and wellness.

## Task 3: Describing Someone's State of Health

Bring your questionnaire with the classmate's, relative's, or friend's answers and your report to class. Exchange the information in groups. Compare your reports to find out about the state of general health of the person you interviewed. Determine which person interviewed seems the healthiest, the least healthy, and why.

## Task 4: Surveying the Class

As a class, find out which person interviewed is the healthiest. Rank order them based on the groups finding's. Record the information on the board.

# KEEP A JOURNAL

## React to Issues

Choose one of the following to write about:

1. Your general state of health.

2. Your eating habits.

3. Your good/bad habits.

4. Any issue related to the topic **Health and Wellness.**

# GO BEYOND THE UNIT THEME

## Improve Your Writing Skills Even More

Now you have an opportunity to write about other topics not related to the topic **Health and Wellness**. Use the same essay pattern you already practised in this unit.

Write an essay on one of the following topics:

- means of transportation
- places we live in (apartment, house, room, etc.)
- different kinds of art that we enjoy
- a topic of your or your teacher's choice

# Unit 4

# Adulthood

**After completing this unit you will be able to**

- analyze a classification essay;
- classify people, things, places, concepts into appropriate categories;
- write classification essays;
- write a variety of introductory paragraphs.

# GET READY

## The Nature of Friendship

> "A friend is someone we like and who likes us. We trust our friends. We share good and bad times with them. We want to be with them and we make time for that purpose. Or, as one armchair philosopher observed, a real friend is one who will continue to talk to you over the back fence even though he knows he's missing his favourite television program."

### Task 1: Let's Make a List

Make a list of as many other "ideals" that we hold for friendships as you can think of. Then compare your list with the rest of the class.

### Task 2: Let's Freewrite

Take 15 minutes and freewrite on the topic of friendship. Using your list, try to define the term "friendship" in the paragraph. Then, share your definition of friendship with the rest of the class.

### Task 3: Interpret the Figure

Look at the following figure of A Common Pattern of Friendship and Acquaintance. Answer the questions in groups of four.

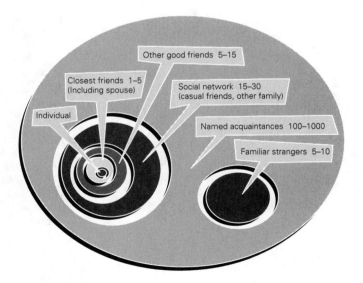

From S. Beebe et al., *Interpersonal Communication*, (Scarborough, ON, 1997), 402, adapted with permission of Prentice Hall Allyn & Bacon Canada.

1. Determine how many types of friendships are listed, and how many people on an average do we know and associate with. (Halve the range to get an average.)

2. Think of all the people that you know, and write an approximate number of closest friends, other good friends, social network, etc. that you know and associate with. Does your number total the average number suggested in the figure?

3. Would you add any other category of friends that hasn't been listed in the figure? If so, which one?

# ANALYZE

## Task 1: Analyzing the Main Ideas and Supporting Information

Read the following essay about different types of friendship. Then answer the following questions:

1. What does "social network" mean?

2. What kinds of friends does the writer talk about? How does he define friendship?

3. What is the difference between acquaintances and casual friends or casual friends and close friends? Use examples to illustrate your point.

4. How many acquaintances, casual friends, and close friends do we have on average?

5. What does the writer mean when he talks about the "level of intimacy"? Explain the term and use a specific example to illustrate.

6. The writer states that most often our closest friends are our own gender. Why is this so? Can we be friends with the opposite sex? Explain your point of view.

7. Why do we need friendships?

## Sample Essay: The World of Friends

George Washington observed, "True friendship is a plant of slow growth, and must undergo and withstand the shocks of adversity before it is entitled to the appellation." Although some of our friendships do blossom suddenly, most proceed through a series of steady and predictable stages, and not all of them become intimate. The intensity of our affection for our friends and the intimacy of our conversations determines whether we view someone as an acquaintance, a casual friend, or a close friend.

Most of us have many acquaintances—people who we know but do not consider friends. For example, we do not send them birthday cards or write them postcards when we travel. Depending upon our occupation and daily activities, we may have dozens of acquaintances. Some people report having more than one thousand acquaintances. If at one point we need these people as our friends, they will become one's. Also, communication with acquaintances tends to be functional and superficial. We may talk with them about school, work, or what we have done or will do over a holiday or weekend. As we do in the early stages of a friendship, when we speak to acquaintances, we limit our self-disclosure to facts keeping our feelings and attitudes to ourselves.

The second type of friends is casual friends. The key difference between acquaintances and casual friends is the level of intimacy in our conversations. We are more likely to reveal personal information to a casual friend than to an acquaintance. For instance, we may have many acquaintances at school, but we would meet with a small group of people to study together. This study group may eventually begin to do such things as have a meal together or go to a movie or a concert. We move from being acquaintances to being casual friends. Casual friends are more likely to volunteer to help one another in time of need. They also are more likely to plan get-togethers than to depend upon chance meetings in the street or at the movies. Casual friends are part of a social network that may also include relatives.

The last type of friendship includes our close friends. As the name implies, they are near and dear to us. They may literally live close to us, or they may move miles away from us. At one time, however, we were interacting with our close friends frequently. More often than not, our closest friends are people of our gender. Often, our conversations with close friends are highly intimate. We confide in those we trust. We also try to see them often. Close friends are those that help the most when we are stressed or troubled. We enjoy their company when all is well; when we have problems, our close friends want to help ease our burdens and pain.

Achieving intimacy is not the goal of all of our friendships. Attempts to force it or to manipulate others in the hopes that they will cling to us and no one else usually backfire. People don't like to be smothered. True friendships are more likely to blossom when the relationship evolves naturally in small increments, when trust is high, and when both individuals have the freedom to make decisions about the relationship. In other words, we should maintain all three types of relationships. Having many acquaintances, a number of casual friends, and a few closest friends is the healthiest approach to relationships.

From S. Beebe et al., *Interpersonal Communication*, (Scarborough, ON, 1997), 409–10, adapted with permission of Prentice Hall Allyn & Bacon Canada.

## Task 2: Classifying Information

Classify the types of friendship and the corresponding characteristics in the chart below.

# Friendship

| Acquaintances | Casual Friends | Closest Friends |
| --- | --- | --- |
| | | |

## Task 3: Stating an Opinion

1. How do you feel about what you read? Do you agree or disagree with the writer's choice of main categories for friendship? Why?

2. List some other categories of friends that the writer did not address that you believe are also important.

3. Can you think of some interesting examples and details about different kinds of friends that the writer could have included in his essay? List them.

# LEARN TO WRITE EFFECTIVELY

## Introductory Paragraphs

An introductory paragraph is a special kind of a paragraph. Its function is to acquaint the reader with the subject of the essay and get the reader's attention. Unless you get the reader's attention, the rest of the essay is wasted. Therefore, to write an interesting and effective introduction, first it is important to write a few sentences that draw the reader into the topic of your essay, and then present the argument through a thesis statement that contains the topic and the ideas to be developed.

There are a number of different ways to grab your reader's attention when writing an introductory paragraph.

1. *You may want to tell a story.* Stories are an interesting way to appeal to the reader's curiosity. They should be brief and related to the main idea (the thesis statement). They can be your personal stories or something you read or heard about.

2. *You could start by describing a situation or an incident.* The reader can relate to situations or incidents that illustrate clearly your point of view. They serve as examples and help the reader recognize the problem more readily.

3. *You might use facts and statistics.* This is another common way to hook the reader. However, it is important to use facts or statistics that startle the reader because he or she does not expect this kind of information, and the facts or statistics must be from a credible source.

4. *You could ask one or more questions.* You may want the reader to think about possible answers or may want to answer those questions yourself.

5. *You may want to use quotations.* This is another way to attract your reader's attention. Quoting someone famous, using a proverb, a favourite expression or a slogan is expressing your ideas through someone else's voice.

No matter which approach you take, make sure that your introductory sentences are related to the thesis statement. It is not a good idea to have a great gap between these two parts. Therefore, having a transition sentence to connect the two parts is very useful; it brings them closer together. In summary, an introduction prepares the reader for your essay, it gets his/her attention, and it states the topic of your essay and the direction it is going to take.

## Task 1: Identifying Introductory Paragraphs

Let us look at some introductory paragraphs. What kind of introduction is it? Identify the attention-grabber. Underline the thesis statement.

1. What is friendship? How do we know who our real friends are? What is the difference between a real friend and someone who we meet casually? What about the many people that we know superficially as acquaintances? How do we relate to these different people? How do we recognize those who will be our friends forever and others whose names we can't even remember? Friendship, as we all know, is not easy to define. However, the intensity of our affection for our friends and the intimacy of our conversations determine whether we view someone as an acquaintance, a casual friend, or a close friend.

2. Charlie was a bright boy who loved his parents despite the violence that occurred in their household. Every time the yelling and fighting would start, Charlie would hide in a small closet. It was impossible not to hear them yelling and screaming at each other. When he was much younger, he always got in the way and ended up being kicked, slapped, pushed around, and yelled at. The cuts and bruises taught him to stay away from his parents when they were at each other's throats. Charlie learned how to protect himself because he realized very early on what kind of family he belonged to. However, it is hard for most children to understand their parents' relationships in conflict situations. There are those who resolve conflict by simply walking away from it, those who fight using physical and psychological abuse, and those who resolve it by sitting down and discussing the conflict.

3. Late last night my friend called to ask if she could come over to talk to me about something extremely personal. We had known each other for some time. We were good friends and knew each other very well. I was a bit confused and worried, but I said, "Sure, come over. What are friends for?" Aisha was pale and in tears when I opened the door. She hugged me and told me that she was getting married. I was completely stunned and speechless. She then told me about a young man who had a bright future, whose family was well established in the community, who was at the right age for marriage, who was looking for a well-educated wife from a respectable family like his own. Aisha had just completed her degree

and "needed" to settle down, as her parents put it. The two families knew each other from way back and decided that this marriage would be good for everyone concerned. Aisha was to meet this young man tomorrow afternoon in the presence of both families. She said through tears that she loved her boyfriend Adam and that she would elope with him immediately. This story is one of thousands illustrating different types of marriages in different societies. In some societies it is natural for the family to arrange a child's marriage while in others the child finds his or her own partner. In other words, there are two types of marriages, arranged marriages and love marriages.

4. Today, most families with two wage earners must entrust their young children to the care of someone else for most of the day. Research shows that nearly 50 percent of children under age 5 in North America are now being cared for outside their own homes. What are possible options for childcare? The most common arrangements are a day-care centre, a live-in baby sitter, or the extended family.

## Task 2: Identifying and Writing an Introduction

1. Now read the introduction of the sample essay and determine what sort of introduction it is. Underline the thesis statement.

2. Go back to Unit 3, Health and Wellness, on page 54 and 55, and develop an introductory paragraph for each thesis statement using one of the approaches above in order to get a reader's attention.

# A Classification Essay

The sample essay is an example of **classification**. College and university students are often asked to organize information into categories or groups. Typically in a classification essay, the writer chooses to focus on grouping characteristics that have something in common. In other words, you can group objects, people, places, events, concepts, etc. that are similar into categories. For example, you can group people on the basis of their personality, age, attitudes, or professions. You can classify food into fruits, vegetables, cereals, meat and fish, dairy products, etc., or foods you eat for breakfast, lunch, and dinner. You can classify movies into horror, dramas, comedies, musicals, etc.

Classification helps you present information clearly and helps the reader to better understand the information presented in your essay. Keep in mind that the concepts grouped together should have many common characteristics in order to make sense to the reader why they fall into the same category. In other words, it is important to select only one basis for classification.

When you write your classification essay, remember that your thesis statement in the introduction determines the categories to be discussed, while each body paragraph discusses a separate category in the order presented in the thesis statement. The concluding paragraph simply summarizes the categories introduced and developed in your essay. No new categories should be established at this point in your writing.

## Typical Transition Words and Expressions for Classification Essays

Transition words used to classify, categorize, or divide information are the same as ordering by number.

the first category, type, group, kind, class

the second category, type, group, kind, class

the third category, type, group, kind, class

the last category, type, group, kind, class

first of all

secondly

the next category, etc.

finally

Other useful expressions used to classify information:

Friends can be **grouped** into three **categories**

| | |
|---|---|
| **classified** | **groups** |
| **categorized** | **types** |
| **organized** | **classes** |
| **divided** | **kinds** |

## Task 1: Identifying Transition Words

Go back to the sample essay and circle all the transition words and classification expressions.

## Task 2: Completing the Sample Outline

Now read the sample essay more carefully to complete the following outline. Compare your finished outline to a partner's outline.

# Sample Outline

**Title:** _____

Introduction/Hook:

_____

_____

Thesis Statement:

_____

_____

A. Paragraph 1 Topic Sentence:

_____

_____

Supporting Statements and Examples:

_____

_____

B. Paragraph 2 Topic Sentence:

_____

_____

Supporting Statements and Examples:

_____

_____

C. Paragraph 3 Topic Sentence:

_____

_____

Supporting Statements and Examples:

_____

_____

Conclusion:
_____

_____

# WRITE

## Brainstorm Together

### Task 1: What Kind of Love is It?

Work in groups and read and discuss the conversations below.

There are different kinds of love that we experience in different types of relationships. Determine what kind of love and type of relationship these people are in. Write down the classification using appropriate terms for each. For example, number 2 below illustrates love as a game. The partners are having fun and not taking their relationship too seriously.

1. **He:** Your eyes. I could get lost in your eyes. And your laugh. I feel so alive when I'm with you. I want to make love to you.
   **She:** Yes. When I'm with you I feel this great desire sweep over me. You take my breath away. I want you more than anything.

2. **He:** Phoebe, I'd like to take you bowling Saturday night if you've never been. It's such a gas at those lanes across town where they still do the setups by hand.
   **She:** Terrific idea. I'll put on my mom's poodle skirt for you. Then later we can go by the lake and park.

3. **She:** Allen, I have to talk with you about Clara. She's acting as if she wants to get rid of me.
   **He:** I know she's been really tense lately about taking her licensing exam. She hasn't been all that nice to me, either.
   **She:** Really? You know, I so appreciate being able to call you up to talk about it.

4. **He:** You know I can't live without you, Darla. Why do you treat me so mean?
   **She:** Baby, it's in my bones. You know I love you, but I need a little freedom, too. I'm just going out with my pal. I'll be back to give you all my love in a few hours.
   **He:** I can't let you go. I just don't believe you when you say you love me. Who is this friend, anyway?

5. **He:** Look, you have two kids, a lousy job, and no husband. I make more money than I know what to do with, I love kids, and I love bungee jumping just as much as you do. Why don't we get married?
   **She:** But I don't love you, Harold. Doesn't that matter?
   **He:** You'll start to love me if you get to know me. Believe me, I'm a great guy.

6. **He:** I hate you, Mommy! You're always saying I can't do this, I can't do that. It's not fair! I hate you!
   **She:** Well, I can understand why you feel that way about me now. But I still love you. Would you like to come read a story with me instead of throwing those marbles in the toilet? We can cuddle up and maybe you'll feel better.
   **He:** No! I hate you!
   **She:** Well, you let me know when you want me to read to you.

Using your notes from the group discussion, complete the chart below by selecting any three types of love you would like to write about and adding the corresponding details:

| Friendship | | |
|---|---|---|
| Love between two friends | | |
| Trust | | |
|  | | |

## Task 2: Kinds of Marriage

Continue working in groups. Discuss the following questions and take notes to use in your essay.

1. What types of marriages do we encounter in the world today? Make a list of different kinds of marriages or permanent relationships between people. To help you make this list, talk about marriages that you personally know about, or that you've heard or read about.

2. Describe different kinds of marriages. How do they differ? Provide some specific examples such as your marriage (if you are married), your parents', your relatives', or your friends' marriages.

Using the notes from the group discussion, complete the chart below by choosing three categories of marriages/permanent relationships and add the corresponding characteristics.

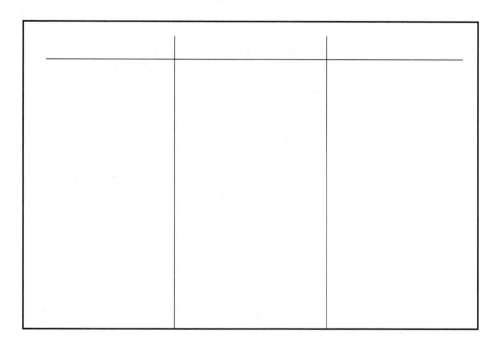

## Task 3: Parenting Styles

In your group, read the following situations, discuss each, and make notes. What kind of relationships do these parents have with their children? As a class with your teacher, try to classify different parenting styles based on these three situations.

1. **Parent:** You can't do that because I say so. Go to your room this instant or you'll be punished. I don't want to hear another word from you, young man. I've had enough of this to last me a lifetime. Get lost right now. (The parent is ready to beat the child).

2. **Parent:** We discussed this already. I think we explained the situation to you. Let's sit down and talk it over.
   **Child:** You said that I could go to the movies with Marc once I finished my assignment. I went over it a few times, and I think it's fine.
   **Parent:** That's not the problem. We agreed that you go to the movies on the weekend and not during the week. Why are the rules being changed without a discussion?

**Child:** Sorry, I forgot. But can I still go this time since I finished my work? I know that this wasn't agreed on and I won't try this again, but the movie we wanted to see is playing only tonight and it's a classic, actually one of your favourites. Maybe you wanted to see it again, too.

3. **Child:** Can I go out now? I'm so bored. There's nothing to do in this house. I wanna hang out with my friends.
   **Parent:** What did you say, honey? I'm still on the phone, I can't hear you from here. Come, darling!
   **Child:** I wanna go out, I said.
   **Parent:** I don't think it's a good idea, but you decide.
   **Child:** Last time you let me go. Now you say it's not a good idea. You never stick to anything you say. Anyway, I'm going. I'll call later or be home in a couple of hours.
   (Six hours later the child is still out and never called as promised).

Use your notes from the group discussion to complete the chart below by selecting three different parenting styles and adding the corresponding supporting information.

|  |  |  |
|---|---|---|
|  |  |  |

# Choose a Topic

1. Choose three different kinds of love that people can experience. Describe each type and provide sufficient details and examples.

2. What are current trends in family life? What are some types of family arrangements that exist today? Write about three different kinds of "marriages" or "permanent relationships" that people are in.

3. Classify parents according to a particular parenting style.

4. Classify any other kind of relationship between people that you are very familiar with or knowledgeable about. For example, types of neighbours, classmates, teachers, etc.

## Start the Writing Process

**Brainstorming.** You have completed this phase in group work. Just add anything that comes to mind at this point that you think you may need and use.

**Selection.** Go over your notes very carefully and select the main ideas that you can develop effectively with examples.

**Development.** Develop the ideas that you have selected. Provide examples for each main idea.

**Organization.** Use the outline form provided below to organize the ideas for your essay. If necessary, refer to the sample outline to help you.

---

## My Classification Essay

Title: _____

Introduction/Hook:

_____

_____

Thesis Statement:

_____

_____

A. Paragraph 1 Topic Sentence:

_____

_____

Supporting Statements and Details:

_____

_____

B. Paragraph 2 Topic Sentence:

_____

_____

Supporting Statements and Details:

_____

_____

C. Paragraph 3 Topic Sentence:

_____

_____

Supporting Statements and Details:

_____

_____

Conclusion:

_____

_____

**Peer Checking.** In pairs, show your outlines to each other. Discuss aspects of the outline that are appropriate and make comments and suggestions about those parts that are unclear, incomplete, or inappropriate.

When evaluating your partner's outline, make sure that

- there are three main ideas;
- each main idea is appropriately developed and clearly supported by examples and details;
- there is a general balance to the discussion of each idea.

**Revision.** Take note of the comments and suggestions made by your partner and use them to revise your outline.

# Grammar Highlights Box

The following grammar structures will help you put your ideas together effectively and edit your work.

**Simple Present**

Communication with acquaintances *tends* to be functional and superficial.

The second type of friends *is* casual friends.

We *move* from being acquaintances to being casual friends.

We *confide* in those we *trust*.

**Modals**

Depending upon our occupation and daily activities, we *may* have dozens of acquaintances.

We *may* have many acquaintances at school, but we *would* meet with a small group of people to study together.

We *should* maintain all three types of relationships.

**Compound Sentences**

They may literally live close to us, *or* they may move miles away from us.

**Complex Sentences**

*Although some of our friendships do blossom suddenly*, most proceed through a series of steady and predictable stages.

*If at one point we need these people as our friends*, they will become friends.

We enjoy their company *when all is well; when we have problems*, our close friends want to help ease our burdens and pain.

## Task 4: Practising Grammatical Structures

Go back to the sample essay and identify other sentences that contain the grammatical structures illustrated in the Grammar Highlights Box.

## Task 5: First Draft

Use your revised outline to write the first draft of your essay.

1. Concentrate on the content and organization and development of ideas.

2. Make sure you have an interesting and appropriate introduction.

3. Don't forget a conclusion.

## Task 6: Second Draft

Read your draft carefully and check for

- choice of vocabulary
- appropriate transition words
- correct grammar
- punctuation
- spelling

## Task 7: Peer Evaluation

Work in pairs. Exchange your essay and complete the Peer Evaluation Form. Then review your partner's comments about your essay and make the necessary changes.

---

# Peer Evaluation Form

**Writer's Name:**

**Evaluator:**

| | Yes | No | If not, please comment |
|---|---|---|---|
| ORGANIZATION | | | |
| 1. The introduction grabs my attention. | | | |
| 2. The thesis statement | | | |
| is clear | | | |
| includes three parallel ideas | | | |
| 3. Each paragraph contains | | | |
| a clear topic sentence | | | |
| supporting details and examples | | | |
| appropriate transitions | | | |
| 4. The conclusion summarizes the main idea of the essay. | | | |

| | Yes | No | If not, please comment |
|---|---|---|---|
| CONTENT | | | |
| 1. The choice of ideas is | | | |
| interesting | | | |
| appropriate | | | |
| clearly stated | | | |
| convincing | | | |
| well illustrated | | | |
| GRAMMAR AND MECHANICS | | | |
| 1. Circle or underline any mistakes that you notice in | | | |
| spelling | | | |
| punctuation | | | |
| grammar | | | |

## Task 8: Final Version

1. Write the final version of your essay.

2. Use the Peer Evaluation Form to double-check your work for weaknesses or errors.

3. Proofread your essay before you hand it in.

# EDIT

## Editing 1

There have been 12 errors introduced into the following text. Correct for errors in

- number
- article
- verb tense
- word form

Unlike childhood and adolescence, <u>adult</u> is not marked by clear, predictable milestones. Still, there are certain <u>experience</u> and changes that nearly everyone goes through and certain needs that nearly everyone tries to fulfill.

Almost every adult forms __ long-term loving partnership with at least one other adult at some point during his or her life. More than 90 percent of all Americans eventually get <u>marry</u> although they are waiting longer to do so. Most people select a marriage or cohabitation <u>partners</u> of similar race, religion, education, and background. According to Erikson, people are not ready for love until they <u>achieved</u> a firm sense of identity. Evidence in favour of <u>Erikson</u> view is the fact that marriages between people who are still in their teens are <u>least</u> successful than those between older people.

___ adult's thinking is more flexible and practical than an adolescent's. Whereas adolescents search for the one "correct" solution to a problem, adults realize that there may be several "right" <u>solution</u> or none at all. Adults place less faith than adolescents in authorities.

No doubt these changes in adult thinking derive from greater experience of <u>a</u> world. Dealing with the kinds of complex problems that <u>arose</u> in adult life requires moving away from the literal, formal, and somewhat rigid thinking of adolescence and young adulthood.

From C. Morris, *Understanding Psychology*, (Scarborough, ON, 1996), pp 332, 343, adapted with permission of Prentice Hall.

# Editing 2

There have been 14 errors introduced into the following text. Edit for errors in

- subject-verb agreement
- verb form
- number
- word form

Robert Sternberg proposes a three-component *triangular theory of love*. The three component are intimacy, passion, and commitment. Sternberg propose that these three components, singly or in various combinations, produce seven differents kinds of love:

*Liking* has only one of the love components—intimacy. In this case, liking is not used in a trivial sense. Sternberg says that this intimate liking characterize true friendships, in which we feel a bondedness, a warmth, and a closeness with another person but not intense passions or a long-term commitment.

*Infatuated love* consists solely of passion and is often what we feel as "love at first sight." But without the intimacy and the decision/commitment components of love, infatuated love may disappears suddenly.

*Empty love* consists of the decision/commitment component without intimacy or passion. Sometimes a stronger love deteriorates into empty love—the commitment remains, but the intimacy and passion have died. In cultures in which arrange marriages are common, relationships often begin as empty love.

*Romantic love* is a combination of intimacy and passion. Romantic lovers are bonded emotionally (as in liking) and physical through passionate arousal.

*Fatuous love* has the passion and the decision/commitment components but not the intimacy. This type of love can be exemplified by a whirlwind courtship and marriage in which a commitment are motivated largely by passion without the stabilizing influence of intimacy.

*Compassionate love* consist of intimacy and commitment. This type of love is often found in marriages in which the passion have gone out of the relation-ship, but a deep affection and commitment remains.

*Consummate love* is the only type that has all three components—intimacy, passion, and decision/commitment. It is the more complete form of love, and it represents the ideal love relationship for which many people strive but which apparently few achieve. Sternberg cautions that maintain a consum-mate love may be even harder that achieving it.

Sternberg stresses the importance of translating the components of love into action. "Without expression," he warns, "even the greatest of loves to die."

From E. Green Wood et al., *The World of Psychology*, (Scarborough, ON, 1996), pp 329–30, adapted with permission of Allyn & Bacon.

# EXTEND YOURSELF

## Task 1: Researching Information

The topic you are to research is **Conflict.** Go to the university/college library and find introductory texts to psychology and interpersonal commu-nication to help you answer the following questions and write a classifica-tion essay. To support the main ideas, search for appropriate examples. You can use personal information or the information you read or heard about.

1. What is conflict? Why do people argue or fight over issues? What are some of the factors that cause conflict rather than cooperation?

2. A conflict can be classified as a disagreement, dispute, campaign, lawsuit, or fight. Describe each and provide specific examples.

3. Do men and women deal with conflict situations differently? You may want to ask some of your classmates how they respond to conflict in order to find out whether they react similarly. Ask them to explain their views and give examples of what they mean. Jot down your findings.

4. Look at these three categories of conflict: (1) pseudo conflict—triggered by a lack of understanding; (2) simple conflict—stemming from different ideas, definitions, perceptions or goals; and (3) ego conflict—based upon personal differences. Try to find some answers to these three categories in psychology and interpersonal relationships and communication texts.

   Take notes on each, including examples.

5. Another division of conflict is (1) constructive and (2) destructive conflict. What is the difference between these two types of conflict? In which situations do people tend to use constructive or destructive strategies?

   From S. Beebe et al., *Interpersonal Communication*, (Scarborough, ON, 1997), pp 291–94, adapted with permission of Prentice Hall Allyn & Bacon Canada.

## Task 2: Writing a Classification Essay

Read through all your answers to the above questions and select the aspect of conflict that interests you the most and for which you have collected sufficient information. Then write a classification essay about it.

## Task 3: Sharing the Story

Bring your finished essay to class. Share it in groups of three. Discuss which essay of the three is most effective, and why. Then read that essay to the rest of the class.

# KEEP A JOURNAL

## React to Issues

Something to write about

1. What kind of personal relationship are you in? What sort of personal relationship is your best friend or a person you admire in?

2. Think of a relationship in which you quarreled, became angry, and lost your cool.

3. Think about three stages of adulthood—adolescence, middle adulthood, and late adulthood. Describe each stage. Which one are you at, and how do you feel about that stage?

4. Any issue related to the topic **Adulthood.**

# GO BEYOND THE UNIT THEME

## Improve Your Writing Skills Even More

Now you have an opportunity to practise writing about other topics other than **Adulthood.** However, it is a good idea to use the same writing pattern you have learned in this unit.

Write a classification essay on one of the following topics:

- kinds of animals/plants/people
- types of foods you love/hate
- kinds of weather conditions/pollution
- a topic of your or your teacher's choice

# Unit 5

# Language and Communication

**After completing this unit you will be able to**

- analyze a comparison and contrast essay;

- categorize similarities/differences using "block" and "point" methods;

- write comparison and contrast essays;

- write a variety of concluding paragraphs.

# GET READY

## Task 1: Let's Freewrite

Take 15 minutes and freewrite how you feel about the English language, how your language is different from English, and how you feel about your English skills. What kind of a language learner are you? Do you like to study grammar or is it more important to you to practise speaking for example? Do you like to read in English or do you always have to have a dictionary by your side?

## Task 2: Let's Compare Spoken and Written Language

Answer the following questions and complete the chart below by yourself. Then check with a partner or a group and add new information to your list. Finally, discuss your lists with the rest of the class.

1.  In learning English, what has been easier for you, speaking or writing in English? Are your speaking skills better than your writing skills or vice versa? Why?

2.  What do you think are some major differences between spoken and written communication?

| Differences | |
| --- | --- |
| Spoken Communication | Written Communication |
| | |

# ANALYZE

## Task 1: Predicting Information

Before you read the essay below, indicate whether the following statements about spoken and written languages are true or false. Mark them either T (True) or F (False). If you believe that the statement is false, write what you think the correct answer is. Check with your partner, then compare the answers to the rest of the class. When you finish reading the essay, come back to this task to check your answers.

_____ Spoken and written language are different in a number of ways.

_____ As young children, we pick up both spoken and written language from our environment.

_____ Spoken language is more difficult to learn than written language.

_____ In order to learn how to write, most children go to school.

_____ Written language is always more formal than spoken language.

_____ In written language, clearly stating a message is crucial.

_____ In both spoken and written language, a message is communicated in the same way.

## Task 2: Stating an Opinion

The following essay compares spoken language to written language. Read the essay and answer the questions below.

## Sample Essay: Spoken and Written Language

Why do most people have no problem talking about an issue, but shy away from conveying the same ideas on paper? Why do students welcome and enjoy conversation classes and group discussions, but groan at the thought of writing essays and research papers? Both spoken and written language are essential for communication; however, the two differ in the learning process, the level of formality, and the communication of meaning.

Spoken and written languages are learned differently. Children learn at a very early age to speak by being exposed to it 24 hours a day in an informal setting. Parents, siblings, extended family, and friends all contribute to children's oral language development. On the other hand, children cannot naturally pick up the skill of writing. Children learn how to write when they are formally taught. School plays a major role in teaching children how to express their ideas in written form. Children who are not formally taught to write remain illiterate.

Another way in which spoken and written language differ is the level of formality. In speaking, there may be no time to produce a "perfect" message. Therefore, a speaker's hesitations, incomplete sentences, self-corrections, and repetitions are a natural part of oral communication. In face-to-face oral communication, the listener's immediate response indicates whether or not the message has been received and comprehended. In contrast, given the formal environment in which writing is learned, certain standards of formality are expected and followed. Clearly stating one's written message is crucial. One cannot assume that there is a shared knowledge with a reader. Therefore, in order for a written message to be effective, it must be organized, coherent, well developed, and accurate. This means there is no room for error and the written message has to be grammatically correct. Whereas what one says is produced immediately, what one writes must go through various stages of revision and editing before its final version.

Finally, spoken messages are reinforced by a wide range of paralinguistic cues, such as facial expressions, body language, tone of voice, and intonation. In face-to-face oral communication, both the speaker and the listener use these to their advantage. However, in written language, there are limited devices available to express different shades of meaning. In order to express an important idea, we might underline, italicize, or bold the message. In addition, punctuation, such as periods, commas, question marks, and exclamation marks are essential in conveying the writer's thoughts.

While both spoken and written language are vital for communication, it is important to recognize that each is learned in different environments, through different methods, and the same message is conveyed and received differently. Thus, most people will agree that it is much easier to exchange information in a conversation rather than to sit down and produce it in written form.

1. How do you feel about what you read? Do you agree or disagree with the writer? Why?

2. What points did the writer address that were similar to yours? Which were different?

## Task 3: Organizing Supporting Information

Read the essay again and complete the chart below, according to the writer's beliefs.

## Differences

| Spoken Communication | Written Communication |
|---|---|
| | |

## Task 4: Analyzing Essay Organization

Work in a group and try to answer the following questions about the organization and development of this essay. Then discuss your answers with the teacher and the rest of the class.

1. What pattern has the writer used to write the essay?

2. Which two issues does the writer identify in her introduction?

3. Which characteristics or aspects of those two issues are being compared? Where in the essay can you find this information?

4. What is the purpose in comparing spoken and written language?

5. How does the writer introduce the topic? How does she conclude it? How are the introductory and the concluding paragraphs similar, and how are they different?

# LEARN TO WRITE EFFECTIVELY

# Concluding Paragraphs

A concluding paragraph is a special kind of a paragraph just like an introductory one. It is the last part of your essay, and it is very important to write it well because it brings your writing to a close and must leave your reader content about the information you presented in your essay. The concluding paragraph has two functions. Its first function is to provide a short summary of the main points by restating the thesis statement in different words. It also must have a final thought-provoking statement or comment on the subject you discussed, so that the reader is encouraged to explore it or think about it further.

Once you have paraphrased your specific key points, there are several ways to finish your essay. You may, for example, want to

- write two or three more general statements on the subject as a whole;
- finish off with a thought-provoking statement or question;
- comment on the future, or predictions about possible outcomes.

Your conclusions may begin with such words as "in conclusion," "to conclude," "in summary," "in sum," "thus," "so," etc.

Note: Always re-read your introduction before you start writing the concluding paragraph.

Avoid repeating every key point you wrote in the essay, changing your point of view, bringing in new ideas, or sounding unsure of yourself.

## Task 1: Identifying Concluding Paragraphs

Read the following concluding paragraphs. Determine what kind of a conclusion it is. Underline the summary of the key points and identify the type of ending the writer uses in the essay. The three most common ways to conclude an essay are

- a thought-provoking statement
- predictions about possible outcomes
- move from specific to general statements

1. Despite such accomplishments, the language skills of chimps, dolphins, and a few other animals are limited. And even specially trained animals cannot, on their own, teach language skills to others of their kind. But the demonstrated language skills of Kanzi and others caution us against assuming that humans alone can lay claim to culture.

2. In sum, symbols allow people to make sense of their lives, and without them human existence would be meaningless. Manipulating symbols correctly allows us to readily engage others within our own cultural system. In a world of cultural diversity, however, the use of symbols may give rise to embarrassment and even conflict.

3. Language skills not only link us with others and with the past but also set free the human imagination. By connecting symbols in new ways, we can conceive of an almost limitless range of future possibilities. Language—both spoken and written—distinguishes human beings as the only creatures who are self-conscious, mindful of our limitations, and aware of our ultimate mortality. Yet our symbolic power also enables us to dream, to envision a better world, and to work to bring that world into being.

4. In short, Wolf asserts, beauty is as much about behaviour as appearance. The myth holds that the key to women's personal happiness lies in beauty (or, for men, in possessing a beautiful woman). In fact, however, beauty amounts to an elaborate system through which society teaches both women and men to embrace specific roles and attitudes that place them in a social hierarchy.

5. Yet strong opposition to feminism persists. Gender still forms an important foundation of personal identity and family life, and it is deeply woven into the moral fabric of our society. Therefore, attempts to change cultural ideas about the two sexes will continue to provoke opposition. On balance, however, while change is likely to proceed incrementally, the movement toward a society in which women and men enjoy equal rights and opportunities seems certain to gain strength.

6. You may think that stealing a sister's husband, or selling off the father's estate and business while he is still alive, or kicking out a sixteen-year-old son because of his unbearable behaviour are extreme examples of family conflicts—right? But how often have your emotions gotten out of control?

From J. Macionis et al., *Sociology*, (Scarborough, ON, 1997), pp. 67, 64, 66, 340, 366, adapted with permission of Prentice Hall Allyn & Bacon Canada.

## Task 2: Identifying and Writing a Conclusion

1. Now read the concluding paragraph of the sample essay and determine what sort of conclusion it is. Underline the summary of the key points and identify the type of ending.

2. Then write an alternative concluding paragraph. Share your paragraph in a group.

3. Go back to Unit 4, Adulthood, page 73, and read the four introductory paragraphs again. Then develop a concluding paragraph for each introduction using one of the three ways to conclude your essay discussed on page 96 in Unit 5.

# A Comparison/Contrast Essay

The sample essay is an example of **comparison/contrast**. This type of essay compares and contrasts the similarities and differences between people, things, or points of view. The same characteristics are discussed for each point of view. Ensure that each characteristic is equally developed and supported by objective information and examples.

Typically in a comparison/contrast essay the writer chooses to focus on either the similarities or differences or a combination of both. Initially, most students, when writing a comparison/contrast essay, find it easier to concentrate on one or the other (i.e., similarities or differences).

Comparison/contrast essays follow different kinds of methods of organization. They may follow either a "block method" or a "point method."

# The "Block" Method

With a block method you concentrate on the first issue or subject and provide all of the supporting statements and details that relate to that issue or subject. When you finish with issue or subject one, you then use the same procedure with the second issue or subject, and so on. Typically, with this approach to essay organization, you will end up with a minimum four-paragraph essay (an introduction, two middle paragraphs, and a conclusion). Read the sample outline below, which illustrates the organization of such an essay.

# Sample Outline:
# Comparison/Contrast
# "Block" Method

Title: _____X/Y_____

Note: Men/Women, Town/City, Cats/Dogs

Introduction/Hook: Men/Women, Town/City, or Cats/Dogs

_____

_____

Thesis Statement: Characteristic 1, Characteristic 2, Characteristic 3 about the two subjects

_____

_____

A. Paragraph 1: Subject 1 + three characteristics/ Topic Sentence:

_____

_____

Supporting Statements and Details for characteristics 1, 2, 3:

_____

_____

_____

_____

_____

B. Paragraph 2: Subject 2 + three characteristics/Topic Sentence:

_____

_____

Supporting Statements and Details for characteristics 1, 2, 3:

_____

_____

_____

_____

_____

_____

Conclusion:

_____

_____

# The "Point" Method

On the other hand, when you use the point method, you write about both issues or subjects together in relation to the first characteristic stated in the thesis statement. Then you write about the same two issues or subjects in relation to the second characteristic, and so on. This means that you go back and forth between those two issues or subjects until you have developed all the characteristics sufficiently. In our example, your essay will have five paragraphs (an introduction, three support paragraphs each developing one characteristic in relation to both subjects, and a conclusion). Look at the outline below, which illustrates the organization of such an essay.

## Sample Outline: Comparison/Contrast "Point" Method

Title: _____X/Y_____

Note: Men/Women, Town/City, Cats/Dogs

Introduction/Hook: Men/Women, Town/City, or Cats/Dogs

_____

_____

Thesis Statement:

_____

Characteristic 1:

_____

Characteristic 2:

_____

Characteristic 3:

_____

A. Paragraph 1/Characteristic 1/Topic Sentence:

_____

_____

Supporting Statements and Details:

_____

X

_____

Transition Word

_____

Y

_____

B. Paragraph 2/Characteristic 2/Topic Sentence:

_____

_____

Supporting Statements and Details:

_____

X

_____

Transition Word

_____

Y

_____

C. Paragraph 3/Characteristic 3/Topic Sentence:

_____

_____

Supporting Statements and Details:

_____

_____

X

_____

Transition Word

_____

Y

_____

Conclusion

_____

# Typical Transition Words for Comparison/Contrast Essays

These words will help you connect your ideas to signal similarities and differences.

| Comparison/Similarities | Contrast/Differences |
| --- | --- |
| similarly | however |
| likewise | on the other hand |
| in the same way | conversely |
| in the same manner | in contrast |
| in addition | but |
| furthermore | on the contrary |
| moreover | nevertheless |
| besides | still |
| in comparison | even though |
| to compare | although |
| also | unlike |
| like | yet, otherwise, whereas |

## Task 3: Identifying Transition Words

Go back to the sample essay and circle the transition words.

## Task 4: Completing the Sample Outline

Now read the sample essay more carefully. Is the essay written using the block or point-by-point method? Complete the outline below and compare it to a partner's outline.

---

# S a m p l e   O u t l i n e :

**Title:** _____

Introduction/Hook:

_____

_____

Thesis Statement:

_____

Characteristic 1:

_____

Characteristic 2:

_____

Characteristic 3:

_____

A. Paragraph 1/Characteristic 1/Topic Sentence:

_____

_____

Spoken Language:

_____

Written Language:

_____

B. Paragraph 2/Characteristic 2/Topic Sentence:

_____

_____

Spoken Language:

_____

Written Language:

_____

C. Paragraph 3/Characteristic 3/Topic Sentence:

_____

_____

Spoken Language:

_____

Written Language:

_____

Conclusion:

_____

_____

# WRITE

## Brainstorm Together

In groups of four, complete the following survey. It is a good idea to take extra notes during the group discussion to help you write your essay later.

|  | You | Student #1 | Student #2 | Student #3 |
|---|---|---|---|---|
| Similarities between your language and English |  |  |  |  |
| Differences between your language and English |  |  |  |  |
| Similarities in how men and women communicate |  |  |  |  |

| | You | Student #1 | Student #2 | Student #3 |
|---|---|---|---|---|
| Differences in how men and women communicate | | | | |
| How would you address these people in an informal setting, such as a party? | | | | |
| friends | | | | |
| parents | | | | |
| president of a company | | | | |
| stranger | | | | |
| grandparent | | | | |
| teacher | | | | |
| Would this change in a formal setting, such as at work or at school? | | | | |

## Choose a Topic

Look at the following list of topics. Select one you would like to write about.

1. How your first language is similar/different to English

2. How men and women communicate in a similar/different manner

3. How levels of formality are similar/different when addressing certain people

## Start the Writing Process

**Brainstorming.** Now that you've selected your topic, brainstorm as many ideas as possible, including both similarities and differences.

**Selection.** Go over your notes very carefully and decide whether your essay will focus on similarities or differences. Select three characteristics that you can develop most effectively.

**Development.** Develop the characteristics that you have selected. Provide supporting statements and details that best illustrate your point of view.

**Organization**. Use the outline form provided to organize the ideas for your essay. Refer to your completed outline.

**Peer Checking**. Show your outline to a partner. Discuss aspects of the outline that are appropriate and make comments and suggestions about those parts that are unclear, incomplete, or inappropriate.

When evaluating your partner's outline, check that

- there are three characteristics being compared/contrasted;
- each characteristic is appropriately developed and clearly supported by examples;
- there is a general balance to the discussion of each characteristic.

**Revision**. Take note of the comments and suggestions made by your partner and use these to revise your outline.

# Grammar Highlights Box

The following grammar structures will help you put your ideas together effectively when you edit your work.

**Simple Present**

Why *do* most people *have* no problem talking about an issue, but *shy away from* conveying the same ideas on paper?

Children *learn* to write when they are formally taught.

While both spoken and written language *are* vital to communication it *is* important to recognize that each is learned in a different environment.

**Passive**

Spoken and written languages *are learned* differently.

In face-to-face communication, the listener's immediate response indicates whether or not the message *has been received* and *comprehended*.

Spoken messages *are reinforced* by a wide range of paralinguistic cues.

**Comparative/Superlative**

Most people will agree that it is *easier* to exchange information in a conversation *than* to sit down and produce it in written form.

## Task 1: Practising Grammatical Structures

Go back to the sample essay and identify other sentences that contain the grammatical structures illustrated in the Grammar Highlights Box.

## Task 2: First Draft

Use your revised outline to write the first draft of your essay.

1. Concentrate on the content, organization, and development of your ideas.

2. Ensure that your introduction includes an interesting hook and a parallel thesis statement.

3. Your conclusion must summarize your major points.

## Task 3: Second Draft

Read your draft carefully and check for

- choice of vocabulary
- appropriate transition words
- correct grammar
- punctuation
- spelling

Make the necessary changes and revise your essay.

## Task 4: Peer Evaluation

Work in pairs. Exchange your essays and complete the Peer Evaluation Form. Then look at your partner's comments about your essay and make any changes.

---

# Peer Evaluation Form

**Writer's Name:**

**Evaluator:**

|  | Yes | No | If not, please comment |
|---|---|---|---|
| ORGANIZATION | | | |
| 1. The introduction grabs my attention. | | | |
| 2. The thesis statement | | | |
| is clear | | | |
| includes three parallel characteristics | | | |

|  | Yes | No | If not, please comment |
|---|---|---|---|
| 3. Each paragraph contains<br><br>a clear topic sentence<br><br>supporting details<br><br>appropriate transitions |  |  |  |
| 4. The conclusion summarizes the main idea of the essay. |  |  |  |
| CONTENT |  |  |  |
| 1. The choice of similarities/ differences is<br><br>interesting<br><br>appropriate<br><br>clearly stated<br><br>convincing<br><br>well illustrated |  |  |  |
| GRAMMAR AND MECHANICS |  |  |  |
| 1. Circle or underline any mistakes that you notice in<br><br>spelling<br><br>punctuation<br><br>grammar |  |  |  |

## Task 5: Final Version

1. Write your final version of the essay.

2. Use the Peer Evaluation Form to double-check for any weaknesses or errors.

3. Proofread your essay before you hand it in.

# EDIT

## Editing 1

There are 10 errors in the following paragraph. Edit for errors in

- verb tense
- verb form
- comparative/superlative

## My Friend and I

I am never good at languages, but I was always a straight-A student in math and science while in high school. These are still my easier subjects now that I'm studying computer science. I've always loved to figure out problems and the trickiest they are, the more interested I am in solving them. I used to spend hours working on my dad's computer when I was a child. Later, in high school, I placed in advanced math and science classes and took part in several municipal, regional, and national competitions. One year, I came first and I award a scholarship to college.

On the other hand, my best friend is into languages all his life. As a child he traveled a lot with his parents and even spent a year at an American school in Switzerland. He has been speaking English, French, and German. We both study at a North American college. He has no problems in his political science courses since his English is perfect. I still struggle with some of my non-science courses and, of course, I must pass the TOEFL test to get into a North American school. Sometimes I am envy my friend, but he says that I'll be quite successful in my profession once I am graduated.

# Editing 2

There have been 10 errors introduced into the following text. Edit for errors in

- word form
- verb tense
- verb form
- subject-verb agreement
- number (singular/plural)
- sentence structure

Time can be used to communicate status. Sophisticate people often make it a point to arrive fashionably late. An early arrival could communicate eagerness and anticipation. Some think it is undignified to be a "keener." If you're concerned about communicating your own personal importance to others. You may think others should eager anticipate your arrival. To wait for others is to place yourself in a diminished position.

We often witness time being used as a status symbol in professional relationship. For example, instructors can arrive late to class and expect no protest. If students arrive late, however, speeches, threats and grade deductions may follow. Also, so-called "important" people may see you by appointment only. While it is permissible for you to drop by without notice on equal status peers and colleagues. Furthermore, although it's allowable for prospective bosses to keep you wait outside their offices, it would not be well-advised for you to show up late for an interview and keep them waiting. That delay should send the wrong message.

Finally, status seems to exempt "important" people from having to endure the waiting that most of us face in life. An acquaintance recently told me of a woman who called her husband restaurant for a reservation. The wait for a table was going to be at least 90 minutes. When the woman identified herself as Dolly Parton, a table was made available immediately. Time talk. In this

> case, it says you're too special and importance to be kept waiting. This may or may not be fair in any objective sense but this seems to be the way it is in the real world.
>
> From A. Falikowski, *Mastering Human Relationships*, (Scarborough, ON, 1996), 310, adapted with permission of Prentice Hall.

# EXTEND YOURSELF

## Task 1: Researching Information

Go to the university/college library and find some information on one of the following topics. You might want to browse through some introductory psychology, sociology, and language texts. Make notes to use later to write your comparison/contrast essay.

1. Compare/contrast two languages in terms of which one is more powerful in today's world.

2. Compare/contrast how men and women communicate in regard to different issues or situations.

## Task 2: Sharing the Story

Bring your finished essay to class. Share it in a group and discuss how effective each essay is, and why. Then read the one essay your group has selected as the most effective, interesting and, in your opinion, well written, to the rest of the class.

# KEEP A JOURNAL

## React to Issues

Choose one of the following to write about:

1. What do you think about your language compared to English?

2. I love my language;

3. The best language in the world;

4. Animals have "language," but it's different from "human" language;

5. Any issue related to the topic **Language and Communication**.

# GO BEYOND THE UNIT THEME

## Improve Your Writing Skills Even More

Now you have an opportunity to practise writing about other topics other than **Language and Communication**. However, it is a good idea to use the comparison/contrast pattern you learned in this unit.

Write a comparison/contrast essay on one of the following topics:

- two people that I admire/love/hate, etc.
- two cities/towns/countries I would live/never live in
- compare your high school life to your university/college life
- a topic of your or your teacher's choice

# Unit 6

# Careers and Professions

**After completing this unit you will be able to**

- analyze a cause-and-effect essay;
- categorize causes and effects and use causal chains;
- write cause-and-effect essays.

# GET READY

## Task 1: Complete Your Resume

First, answer the following questions on your own. Use the form below to record your answers. Record your opinion on a separate sheet of paper. You will need this information to work in a group.

1. How many years of schooling have you had?

2. Which schools have you attended so far? Start from elementary school.

3. Have you attended any other kinds of schools, courses, programs, camps (music, math, computer, sports, art, language, drama, etc.) besides your regular school? What skills have you obtained? Can they be an asset in your future career or occupation?

4. Have you ever volunteered or worked? What kind of work have you done? Will these experiences be valuable and important in your future profession? Why or why not?

5. Do you think your education will be crucial in reaching your professional goals? What are those goals? Do you think you will be more professionally successful because you will be a college or university graduate?

6. What are some of the most important benefits you think you will have in your occupation because of your education? List them.

7. Do you plan to continue educating yourself once you gain your credentials? Why or why not?

---

# My Resume

### Education

1. Number of years in school:

_____

2. Schools attended:

_____

_____

3. Other types of schools and programs:

_____

_____

4. Skills obtained:

_____

_____

## Work Experience

1. Volunteer work:

_____

_____

2. Paid work:

_____

_____

## My Future

Professional goals:

_____

_____

Expected benefits in occupation:

_____

_____

Professional development:

_____

_____

## Task 2: Let's Compare Our Resumes

In your group, compare your answers to find out how similar/different they are. Then, share the findings with the rest of the class.

# ANALYZE

## Task 1: Analyzing the Main Ideas and Supporting Information

The following essay discusses some important benefits of good education. Read the essay and answer the following questions:

1. What are, in the writer's opinion, the most important benefits of good education? Highlight the main ideas.

2. What are some specific examples as to why it is important to go to school and become a professional? Underline them and then discuss the answers with your classmates.

## Sample Essay: Benefits of Good Education

When I was a child, my parents always lectured me and my older brothers on the importance of good education. We were obedient children and we listened to these talks patiently without much understanding. Later, during our teenage years, my brothers and I liked to joke about our parents' seriousness when they talked about school. We imitated them and laughed behind their backs. However, soon after my brothers entered university, I realized how their attitude towards school and learning had changed. There was no more fun in the house. They had joined the ranks of our parents and I was left all by myself to fight for my rights and opinions. However, it did not take me long to realize that my high school diploma did not provide many exciting and well-paying jobs. A year later, after trying to become a famous musician, an efficient sales person, and an irresistible bartender, I was truly defeated. I had to admit that I had made a poor decision, and with my parents' understanding and my brothers' support, I became a university student. It did not take me long to finally comprehend what my parents had been trying to do all those years. I joined my brothers in their belief that good education provides one with many benefits, the most important being greater job and promotion opportunities, higher economic and social status, and greater personal satisfaction.

First and foremost, when a person gains a professional degree, he has many more job opportunities. All companies, large or small, need professionals who can take on responsible positions. They like to hire young graduates who are up to date, enthusiastic, flexible, and not as expensive as their experienced colleagues. Even if a person starts at an entry-level position, he can expect to be promoted after gaining experience and proving himself as an expert in his field. A young doctor usually starts his career as an intern before he can start his own practice. An inexperienced business management graduate will probably start as someone's assistant before she becomes someone else's manager. If a young person has the right qualifications, he can gain necessary experience quickly and, as a result, be promoted to a more demanding position. Furthermore, a person with a university degree can expect to be in a leadership position one day. If a young lawyer works hard to gain the needed expertise in her profession and has the right leadership skills, she may eventually become a court judge. A young mathematician or a physicist may start his career as a teacher, then become a university professor, and finally the university vice-president. In other words, job possibilities are endless for a person who decides to obtain adequate education.

Another important benefit of having good education is enjoying a higher economic and social status. Every young person likes to earn more money in order to have a more comfortable lifestyle. Usually, the salaries of young graduates tend to be higher than those of people who do not hold professional degrees or diplomas. Also, just as there are possibilities for promotions, there are opportunities for salary increases. As a person grows older, he has more financial responsibilities such as a family, a mortgage, a car loan, children's schooling, etc. It is satisfying to know that he can count on an increase in salary. In addition to financial stability, a young person can count on gaining social status and the respect and trust of colleagues and co-workers. If a young person is knowledgeable and hardworking as well as fair and approachable, she will undoubtedly become a member of a professional circle and as a result become more influential. Having a good salary and being important in one's social circle can no doubt be attributed to being well educated.

Lastly, personal satisfaction with one's professional achievements is the greatest benefit. A young person, even when he holds a degree, usually lacks self-confidence and has a low self-esteem because he knows he has neither experience nor maturity. However, this confidence and esteem can be gained simply by taking one's profession seriously and enthusiastically. If he loves his job and knows how to enjoy it while working hard at it, his success is almost guaranteed. If he asks questions and is willing to still learn, is motivated to do a good job every time, likes to work with his co-workers, and likes to see results after a day's work, he will go home happy. He will probably be praised by colleagues, co-workers, and bosses on his great job, and will get good reviews. In other words, professional satisfaction results in personal satisfaction.

In conclusion, everyone should get a good education and reach their goals. My brothers are already working and their experience helps me to push myself as far as I can go. I have realized that being well educated opens many more doors when one is seeking a job, a promotion, a better salary, approval, and respect. This freedom of opportunity results in being content with one's life in general.

## Task 2: Organizing Supporting Information
Read the essay again and complete the chart below.

**Examples of:**

| Professional Opportunities | Status | Satisfaction |
|---|---|---|
|  |  |  |

## Task 3: Analyzing Introductory and Concluding Paragraphs

1. Now read only the introduction. How does the writer start his essay? Why do you think he is using a personal example, (writing in the first person singular "I")? Would the effect be the same if he wrote the same story about someone else? "When John was a child, his parents . . ." Why or why not?

2. How does the writer conclude his essay? What message does he want his readers to get? Why is being well educated important to him?

## Task 4: Stating an Opinion

1. How do you feel about what you read? Do you agree or disagree with the writer's choice of main ideas? Why?

2. List some of the benefits of good education not addressed by the writer, which you believe are also very important.

3. Can you think of some interesting examples that the writer could have included in his essay? List them.

# LEARN TO WRITE EFFECTIVELY

## A Cause-and-Effect Essay

The essay you just read is an example of **cause and effect.** Typically in a cause-and-effect essay, the writer chooses to focus on either the causes or effects or a combination of both. Initially, when you write an essay using this approach, concentrate on either causes or effects because it is easier to control the development of your ideas. Once you have sufficient practice and are required to write longer essays and papers, you can use a combination of both.

You use this type of essay to discuss the causes or reasons that lead to a certain event or situation or explain how the situation or event itself produces effects or consequences. Either could be positive or negative. A typical question you ask yourself when you want to write a cause-and-effect essay is *Why?* or *What?* or *Who?* The answer(s) to these questions will provide you with logical explanations that support your argument. Careful observation, investigation, and examination of the events or situations are essential when writing an effective cause-and-effect essay.

Examples of causes:   Poverty is the cause of poor education.
People cannot find work because of an economic recession.

Examples of effects:   A position I have now is the direct result of my degree.
I dropped out of school when I was 16. Consequently, I couldn't find a decent job to support myself.

A cause-and-effect essay follows an example essay method of organization; that is, your causes or effects are listed in order of importance. If you discuss three causes or three effects of an event or situation, you will provide supporting statements and examples that clearly relate to your main idea.

The cause-effect sentence pattern is often used in this type of essay. It looks as follows:

X causes Y .
X is one of the causes of Y .
The main cause of Y is X .
Y is caused by X .
The most important effect of X is Y .
Y is due to X .
X is a fact. As a result, Y will happen.

This kind of pattern is called **causal chains**. You can use arrows to connect the chain of events to help you analyze more easily whether your ideas are tightly related and logically developed.

# Examples of causal chains:

| Cause | → | Effect |
|---|---|---|
| Bright and hardworking | → | excellent student |
| Skipped a couple of grades | → | high school by age 16 |
| Was admitted to prestigious university | → | had top professors |
| The degree gained | → | wide professional opportunities |
| His knowledge, intelligence, and personal qualities | → | promotions |
| Personal and professional growth | → | personal satisfaction and professional success |

# Typical Transition Words for Cause-and-Effect Essays

These words will help you connect your ideas to signal cause and/or effect.

| Cause | Effect |
|---|---|
| because | as a result |
| cause(s) | result in (from) |
| since | consequently |
| due to | so (that) |
| | therefore |
| (for) the reason (that) | lead to |
| | have an effect on |

## Task 1: Creating Causal Chains

Go back to the sample essay and find the sentences that will help you to create a causal chain diagram. The chain would begin as follows:

As obedient children → listened to our parents lecturing us.
When we became teenagers → we laughed.
My brothers went to university → their attitude to school changed.

Continue tracing and recording this type of sentence.

## Task 2: Completing the Sample Outline

Now, read the essay more carefully to complete the following sample outline. Compare your finished outline to a partner's outline.

---

# Sample Outline

**Title:** _____

Introduction/Hook:

_____

_____

_____

Thesis Statement:

_____

_____

_____

A. Paragraph 1 Topic Sentence:

_____

_____

Supporting Statements and Examples:

_____

_____

_____

B. Paragraph 2 Topic Sentence:

_____

_____

Supporting Statements and Examples:

_____

_____

---

C. Paragraph 3 Topic Sentence:

_____

_____

Supporting Statements and Examples:

_____

_____

_____

_____

Conclusion:

_____

_____

_____

_____

# WRITE

## Brainstorm Together

### Task 1: Let's Talk About Work

In groups of four, discuss the following questions. During the discussion, take extensive notes, which will later help you to write your own essay.

1. How do people choose a career? What is your major/program? How did you decide what to study? Was it on your own or did other people influence you? Who are they? Why did you decide to study? What are your expectations? What do you think the benefits might be? What might be some negative aspects of your future profession?

2. What are some of the reasons people want to be self-employed or own a business? When a person has her own business what could be some advantages or disadvantages? If you wanted to be self-employed or own a firm/business, what would it be and why? What would be some types of self-employed work that you could do in your profession? What would be some important benefits?

3. What is workaholism? Have you ever met a workaholic? What is he like?

Why do you think some people are workaholics? What are some serious consequences of workaholism?

4. Did you or someone you know ever quit a job? Why? Why do people sometimes have to or want to quit their job?

# Choose a Topic

Look at the following list of topics. Select one you would like to write about.

1. Reasons or effects for choosing a particular career/profession

2. Reasons for self-employment or effects of owning a business

3. Consequences of workaholism

4. Causes for quitting a position

## Task 2: Adding Information

Read your notes carefully and decide which of the above topics you would like to write an essay on. Once you have selected your topic, add a few more questions that haven't been discussed in your group but that you need some answers to.

## Task 3: Sharing Ideas on the Same Topic

Now, sit with a group of students who selected the same writing topic. Exchange the information you already have and discuss everyone's new questions. Take more notes.

# Start the Writing Process

**Brainstorming.** Now that you've selected your topic, brainstorm as many ideas as possible, including examples.

**Selection.** Go over your notes very carefully. Select three main ideas that you can develop effectively with examples.

**Development.** Develop the ideas that you have selected. Provide examples with supporting statements and details that best illustrate your point of view.

**Organization.** Use the outline form provided to organize the ideas for your essay. Refer to the sample outline to help you.

---

## My Cause-and-Effect Essay:

Title: _____

Introduction/Hook:

_____

---

_____

_____

Thesis Statement:

_____

_____

_____

A. Paragraph 1 Topic Sentence:

_____

_____

Supporting Statements and Examples:

_____

_____

_____

B. Paragraph 2 Topic Sentence:

_____

_____

Supporting Statements and Examples:

_____

_____

_____

C. Paragraph 3 Topic Sentence:

_____

_____

Supporting Statements and Examples:

_____

_____

_____

Conclusion:

_____

_____

_____

**Peer Checking.** In pairs, show your outlines to each other. Discuss aspects of the outline that are appropriate and make comments and suggestions about those parts that are unclear, incomplete, or inappropriate.

When evaluating your partner's outline, check that

- there are three main ideas;
- each main idea is appropriately developed and clearly supported by examples;
- there is a general balance to the discussion of each main idea.

**Revision.** Take note of the comments and suggestions made by your partner and use these to revise your outline.

# Grammar Highlights Box

The following grammar structures will help you put your ideas together when you edit your work.

**Simple Present**

First and foremost, when a person *gains* a professional degree, he *has* many more job opportunities.

**Simple Past**

When I *was* a child, my parents always *lectured* me and my older brothers about school.

**Past Perfect Simple and Continuous**

I had to admit that I *had made* a poor decision. It did not take me long to finally comprehend what my parents *had been trying* to do all those years.

**Future Will**

This person *will* probably *hear* from colleagues and bosses what a great job he has done.

**Modals**

A young mathematician or a physicist *may* start her career as a teacher.

In conclusion, everyone *should* get good education and reach his goals.

**Complex Sentences: Adverbial Clauses, Adjective Clauses**

*If a young person is knowledgeable and hardworking,* she will undoubtedly become a member of a professional circle.

All companies, large or small, need professionals *who can take on responsible positions.*

**Participial Adjectives**

It did not take me long to realize that my high school diploma did not provide me with *exciting* and well-*paying* jobs.

## Task 4: Practising Grammatical Structures

Go back to the sample essay and identify other sentences that contain the grammatical structures illustrated in the Grammar Highlights Box.

## Task 5: First Draft

Use your revised outline to write the first draft of your essay.

1. Concentrate on the content, organization, and development of ideas.

2. Ensure that your introduction includes an interesting hook and a parallel thesis statement.

3. Your conclusion must summarize your major points.

## Task 6: Second Draft

Read your draft carefully and check for

- choice of vocabulary
- appropriate transition words
- correct grammar
- punctuation
- spelling

## Task 7: Peer Evaluation

Work in pairs. Exchange your essay and complete the Peer Evaluation Form. Then look at your partner's comments about your essay and make the changes to your essay that you think are necessary.

# Peer Evaluation Form

**Writer's Name:**

**Evaluator:**

|  | Yes | No | If not, please comment |
|---|---|---|---|
| **ORGANIZATION** | | | |
| 1. The introduction grabs my attention. | | | |
| 2. The thesis statement | | | |
| is clear | | | |
| includes three parallel ideas | | | |
| 3. Each paragraph contains | | | |
| a clear topic sentence | | | |
| supporting sentences | | | |
| details | | | |
| appropriate transitions | | | |
| **CONTENT** | | | |
| 1. The choice of ideas is | | | |
| interesting | | | |
| appropriate | | | |
| clearly stated | | | |
| convincing | | | |
| well illustrated | | | |

| | Yes | No | If not, please comment |
|---|---|---|---|
| GRAMMAR AND MECHANICS | | | |
| 1. Circle or underline any mistakes that you notice in | | | |
| spelling | | | |
| punctuation | | | |
| grammar | | | |

## Task 8: Final Version

1. Write the final version of your essay.

2. Use the Peer Evaluation Form to double-check your work for weaknesses or errors.

3. Proofread your essay before you hand it in.

# EDIT

......................................................................

## Editing 1

There have been 13 errors introduced into the following text. Edit for errors in

- verb tense
- word form
- verb form

My older sister best friend Linda has worked for a big financial trust for over

three years. A few weeks ago, the company sent a memo informing their

employees that it is upgrading several positions in the management depart-

ment. The attached list of jobs stated the new qualifications that had to

be met. Linda was furious because the new position the company was

opening up—the job she had slanted to get—was listed. She went to see her supervisor and told her that she had been working there for three years, that she had always had good evaluations, and that she was told she will get that new position. The supervisor was sorry and told her that she had highly recommended Linda for the new position. Linda was no doubt a hardworking, responsible, trustworthy and reliable employee. She had great interpersonal skills and colleagues liked her very much. Most importantly, Linda had gained a lot of experience on the job, but unfortunately, it was not her boss's deciding. It was decided by those higher up that a university degree was necessary for this new position. Linda knew she is a year short of her degree in business management, but it was impossible for her to go back to school and study. It has been four years since she was in university. The supervisor was sympathetic, but her hands was tied. Linda would have to continue work at the lower job classification and stay at the lower pay.

It was Linda's responsibility to training Amy, the newcomer with the just gotten university degree. Those were the most difficult two weeks Linda ever spent at work—especially since she knows that Amy was already being pay more than she was.

When I heard the story, I knew then that I will never quit school for anything. Linda must have had a good reason for not finishing her degree then, but it surely was not worth it now. Degrees and diplomas were required by large firms and corporations and if a person is not qualified for a position, no work experience, special skills or personal qualities can replaced one's credentials.

From J. Henslin and A. Nelson, *Sociology*, (Scarborough, ON, 1996), 470, adapted with permission of Prentice Hall Allyn & Bacon Canada.

# Editing 2

There have been 14 errors introduced into the following text. Edit for errors in

- number
- wrong word/word choice
- subject-verb agreement
- word form

- verb form
- verb tense
- article

Who has the higher IQ score ever recorded on an intelligence test? The name of Albert Einstein quickly comes to mind and perhaps a host of other great thinker of the past—mostly men. But the person with the highest IQ score ever recorded happens to be a woman.

Marilyn Mach, born in St. Louis, Missouri, in 1946, scored an amazing 230 on the Stanford-Binet IQ test when she was a 10-year-old elementary school student. How high is a 230 IQ? The average score is set at 100, and a score of 116 place a person in the top 16 percent of a population. Not only does Marilyn Mach have no peers when it come to measured intelligence, she doesn't even have a competitor. Her score is nearly 30 points higher than that of her nearest rival.

Marilyn has no university degree, but she is completed about two years of courses at a community college and a university. She is interesting in creative writing, and she has written twelve books and three plays. Her first published work was the *Omni IQ Quiz Contest*. Marilyn live with her husband in New York, where she writes a newspaper column, lecture on intelligence, and pursues other interests.

Now let us consider Robert Jarvik. Dr. Jarvik combined his medicinel knowledge and his mechanical genius to produce the world's first workable artificial heart. But his life wasn't easy. He was a poor test taker. In fact, he

score too low on intelligence and admissions tests to be admitted to any

medical school in U.S.. Eventually, he received his doctor's degree from a

university in Italy. Then he returned to the U.S. and made his contribution to

medical science—a contribution that kept alive many gravely ill heart patients

until a suitable heart transplant can be performed.

Perhaps, if Dr. Jarvik wishes, he can learn to score higher on IQ tests. His

wife Marilyn Mach had to be willing to teach him.

From Wood et al., *The World of Psychology*, (Scarborough, ON, 1996), 224, adapted with
permission of Allyn & Bacon Canada.

# EXTEND YOURSELF

## Task 1: Interviewing

Research one of the following topics using the **interview method**. Follow
the four steps below.

1. Develop a series of questions for an in-depth interview.

2. Find a person who is already working in the profession you are studying
   for and who is willing to be interviewed.

3. As you ask the questions, take extensive notes to help you write an
   effective report later.

4. Ask for clarification of information as well as for specific examples that
   support the information provided by the interviewee.

## Task 2: Adding Information

Once you have completed the interview, go over your notes and write a
report addressing either causes or effects. Create your own title.

# Choose a Topic

1. The person you interviewed is professionally very successful.
   Find out the reasons for his or her success.

OR

Find out the effects of his or her professional success.

2. The person you interviewed is not satisfied with his or her professional life.
   Find out what has caused his or her dissatisfaction with the profession.
   OR
   Find out the consequences of his or her disappointment in his or her work.

3. The woman you interviewed has been discriminated against in the workplace.
   Find out the causes for this discrimination.
   OR
   Find out the effects on this woman.

### Task 3: Sharing Ideas on the Same Topic

Present your written report orally to your group. As a group, discuss your reactions to each report. Which report is most effective, and why? Then report your discussion to the rest of the class.

# KEEP A JOURNAL

## React to Issues

Choose one of the following to write about:

1. Your dream profession, career, job.

2. Why I don't like certain professions or jobs.

3. Any issue related to the topic **Careers and Professions**.

# GO BEYOND THE UNIT THEME

## Improve Your Writing Skills Even More

Now you have an opportunity to practise writing about topics other than **Careers and Professions.** However, it is a good idea to use the same writing pattern you have learned in this unit.

Write a cause-and-effect essay on one of the following topics:

- causes of poverty/crime/alcoholism, etc.
- the growth of cities and its effects
- the effects of computer technology on our daily lives
- a topic of your or your teacher's choice

# Unit 7

# Science and Technology

**After completing this unit you will be able to**

- analyze a process essay;

- order steps in a process;

- write process essays and reports;

- provide instructions and directions on "how to . . .".

# GET READY

## Task 1: Let's Talk About Science and Technology

Work in groups and discuss the following questions. After group work, discuss them with the rest of the class.

1. What is science? Define the term and give examples.

2. What is technology? Define the term and give examples.

3. Compare and contrast science and technology.

4. Describe the role that scientists play in the use of technology.

5. What roles do science and technology play in our lives?

6. What do you think are some of the most important scientific discoveries of all times? Why?

7. What are the most important technological achievements that you can think of?

8. What is the impact of technology on us and our environment? Which types of technology do we use in our daily lives for communication, transportation, food, clothing, entertainment, etc.?

9. Choose one of the technological gadgets or innovations, make a list of steps on how to use it, and then explain the process to your group. For example, how do we use a telephone, a cell phone, a TV, a bank machine, email, the Internet, a washing machine or a car?

10. How is something made? How is a telescope, a car, or a camera built?

11. For example, let's make a pinhole camera. All the steps are given to you. Put them in the correct order by numbering them.

Part 1

_____ take a cardboard box

_____ take the pinhole camera and aim it at a bright object such as a candle

_____ make a pinhole at the other end of the box

_____ you will see an upside-down image on the tissue paper

_____ cut out one end

_____ darken the room

_____ cover the cut-out end with tissue paper

_____ the pinhole camera is ready to use

Part 2

_____ if you want to take a picture, in complete darkness, replace the tissue
paper with unexposed photographic film

_____ the photographic film is exposed and the picture is taken

_____ aim the camera at the candle

_____ cover the back of the box light cannot get in

_____ remove the lid or flap

_____ light the candle

_____ cover the pinhole with a lid or flap

## Task 2: Let's Write About How Something Is Made

Now that you've determined the order of the steps for making a pinhole
camera, write a process paragraph about it. Include a topic sentence and
a concluding one, and use transition words (first, next, then, now, etc.)
where needed.

# ANALYZE

## Task 1: Analyzing the Main Ideas and Supporting Information

The sample essay below discusses the scientific process. Read the essay for
general content, answer the questions below, and discuss your answers with
the rest of the class.

1. How does the title **The Path of Scientific Development** relate to the
   content of the essay?

2. The author of this article states that human beings are curious. Where
   has this curiosity led humankind so far?

3. How many steps are there in the scientific process? What are they?

4. What is the definition of "hypothesis"? Give an example.

5. Why is it so important in scientific research to be objective? How is this
   objectivity ensured?

6. What do scientists do with the accumulated data in order to find
   patterns in them?

7. How may a hypothesis become a theory? How is the theory confirmed?
   What happens if the theory breaks down?

8. What does the author mean when he says that we use the scientific method throughout our lives? Give an example from your own personal experience.

# Sample Essay: The Path of Scientific Development

Human beings are curious by nature, and it is this very curiosity that has led to much that is admirable in what humankind has produced. Reduced to its core, curiosity is simply asking questions. Why do people behave the way they do? Can people live on other planets in our universe? What if the human brain could be transplanted? Questions like these can lead to new theories in psychology, astronomy and physical sciences, or medicine. However, from asking questions to discovering or creating a theory is a long and rigorous scientific process which consists of the methodical observing of a body of data, determining the relationships and regularities, and figuring out the organizing and underlying patterns and principles.

The cycle of scientific development starts with an idea, a problem to be solved, or a speculation generated out of curiosity. This, in science, is referred to as an **hypothesis.** In response, the first primary activity is set in motion—scientific activity starts with observation. Observations are not just limited to the five human senses. We live in a world with powerful extensions to our primary senses. A simple set of binoculars drastically amplifies our ability to identify a bird in the woods or to see the stars and planets with a clarity that an astronomer of 400 years ago could not even imagine. However, it is not enough to have powerful instruments since scientific observation requires both skill and discipline: the persistence of a keen nature observer waiting for hours to see the mating habits of obscure species, or the technical skill of the operator of a multi-million dollar electron microscope. Finally, every area of scientific observation requires objectivity.

Scientific objectivity should allow one to "see" what is really there and not what one hopes to "see." The ultimate abstract objectivity is achieved when all competent observers agree that they "see" the same thing in the same set of circumstances.

Once a body of data has been accumulated from reliable observation, the next task is to attempt to make some sense and order out of the data in search for regularities, patterns, or laws. This search, whether simple or complex, is a long-term goal of science, and it is carried out by using a variety of methods such as cataloguing samples, making diagrams, creating graphs, using statistical analysis and other powerful mathematical tools. Finding patterns in random data is crucial before creating laws and empirical rules for design and extension to be used by science and society. For instance, using the periodic table of the elements, a chemist can predict that an element in the same column but next row can be expected to have similar properties to the one in the previous row. This may be enough guide or warning to allow one to make a useful compound or avoid a potentially explosive one. At this stage in the path of scientific development we may have some very useful rules for how things work, but we do not know why they work as they do. There appears no obvious fundamental mechanism, only rules, often very complex and arbitrary ones connecting certain facts and events. To simplify and make sense of these rules a scientist is urged to discover an underlying principle.

Finally, the discovery of grand themes and fundamental theories is the greatest achievement of the creative human mind working in the name of science. The laws of universal gravitation, relativity, evolution, and genetics are examples of underlying mechanisms. These themes did not emerge from reason alone. Like artists, scientists must step beyond the structured data and rules and make an educated guess or an intuitive leap that opens a new possibility and a new way of thinking.

However, the scientific process does not stop with a good guess. Rigorous and systematic testing proves whether a creative guess was right or wrong. The fundamental theory is often simple and grounded in an elegant and aesthetically pleasing principle. It looks obvious, right and natural. For instance, Albert Einstein's simple, elegant and powerful $E=mc^2$ is a symbol that is recognized by almost anyone in our century. Finally, the discovery of an underlying mechanism creates new possibilities. It begs to be used and tested in new areas. Great advances in scientific development and technological application take place following the major scientific theory. Applications that work confirm the theory. When the theory begins to break down and special rules and adjustments are needed to get consistent results and a new understanding of the fundamental mechanism is necessary, we are thrown back to the beginning of the scientific process. And the science moves on, never complete, no matter how convincing, powerful and elegant a particular theory may be at one time.

The scientific endeavour is a mammoth undertaking. As we already know, a hypothesis starts the scientific process of observing phenomena, structuring and using the collected data, and discovering and creating an underlying mechanism or a theory. This process of question and answer in science is known as the scientific method. It is a method we all use, to a greater or lesser extent, as we navigate throughout our lives. The degree of rigour used determines how well we learn from our experience and how clearly we see the forces at work in the world around us. As Carl Sagan writes, "Those creatures who find everyday experience a muddled jumble of events with no predictability, no regularity, are in grave peril. The universe belongs to those who, at least to some degree, have figured it out."

From W. Hanna and C. Cockerton, *The Human Project*, (Scarborough, ON, 1996), 205–08, adapted with permission of Prentice Hall.

## Task 2: Transferring of Information

Read the essay again and complete the path of scientific development using note form in the chart below.

---

**The Path of Scientific Development**

**an idea**

_____

**the process**

_____

A. Observing

_____

_____

1.

_____

2.

_____

3. "objectivity"

_____

_____

_____

B. Structuring and using information

_____

_____

1.

_____

2.

_____

3.

_____

_____

C. Discovering/creating an underlying mechanism

_____

_____

1. a creative leap beyond reasoning

_____

2.

_____

3.

_____

## Task 3: Understanding the Scientific Process

Read the essay once more and discuss the following questions with your classmates. State your opinions clearly by providing concrete examples to support your views.

1. What do you think about the essay you just read? What kind of information is the writer providing? In other words, why is this information valid and verifiable?

2. Did you understand the procedure of the scientific method? What happens first, second, third?

3. How does the writer begin and conclude his essay?

## Task 4: Putting It in Order

Put the following information in the correct order and then write a short summary paragraph about the scientific method.

_____ testing a hypothesis

_____ drawing conclusions

_____ reporting results

_____ forming a hypothesis

_____ gathering information

_____ stating a problem

# LEARN TO WRITE EFFECTIVELY

## A Process Essay

The sample essay is a **process** essay. This is a simple essay-writing pattern because you are asked to explain a procedure step by step clearly and logically so that your reader can understand and follow it precisely. This type of essay tells you how something works or is done, or describes how something happens. In the first case, your reader can understand and follow a process by achieving the same result, for example, how to conduct an experiment or a test. In the second, your reader can understand a process but not repeat it; for example, how a movie is made, how a car is manufactured, or how a war began.

It is important to know all of the steps in the process you are to explain. Your knowledge is based on reading or hands-on experience, and it must be thorough so that you can present the order of steps or phases as clearly as possible.

When you write a process essay, you may want to address the content using two different grammatical structures. You can address your reader directly using the personal pronoun "you" and the imperative form or just the imperative without "you." This approach is less formal and more direct, expecting the reader not only to understand the information but also probably perform the process. The other approach to writing a process essay is more formal and usually used by scientists, engineers, computer programmers, etc. who use the passive voice in order to sound more formal and distant. Usually reports of a process are written in this manner. Often, the passive voice tends to be overused especially in technical writings. It is a good idea to use the active voice wherever possible.

Examples:

**Informal**

You should do this; then you should do that. (personal pronoun "you" + imperative)

Do this, do that, then do the other thing. (imperative)

**Formal**

First, the engine is checked, then it is put into the hood. Next, it is connected to the electrical elements in the car, etc. (passive voice)

## Typical Transition Words for Process Essays

These words will help you connect your ideas in the process essay. To show the chronological nature of process writing, the following transitions should be part of your essay:

first, second, third, another, last, final

first, next, then, before, after, while, as, at the same time, at the end, finally

only recently, until, yet, when, by the time, as soon as, since, at the same time, in the meantime, meanwhile, afterwards

**Other useful words when you write a process essay:**

**Nouns:** steps, instructions, directions, method, stage, phase, procedure, process

**Verbs:** start, begin, precede, follow, continue, complete, test, experiment, observe, record, form, formulate, find, control, conclude, report

## Task 1: Identifying Transition Words

Go back to the sample essay and circle all the transition words you can find.

## Task 2: Completing the Sample Outline

Now go back to the sample essay and read it more carefully to complete the following outline. Compare your finished outline to a partner's outline.

# S a m p l e   O u t l i n e

**Title:** _____

Introduction/Hook:

_____

_____

_____

Thesis Statement:

_____

_____

_____

A. Paragraph 1 Topic Sentence:

_____

_____

Supporting Statements and Examples:

_____

_____

_____

B. Paragraph 2 Topic Sentence:

_____

_____

Supporting Statements and Examples:

_____

_____

_____

C. Paragraph 3 Topic Sentence:

_____

_____

Supporting Statements and Examples:

_____

_____

_____

Conclusion:

_____

_____

_____

# WRITE

## Brainstorm Together

Note: You don't need to be an expert to answer the following questions. It is a good idea to gather some information about the processes you will be discussing in your group. The teacher will assign this task before it is taken up in class.

Take 10 minutes to freewrite on question #4. Then work in a group and answer all following sets of questions. Provide sufficient notes to help you later write a process essay on one of the topics listed below. Try to list all the steps of the process.

1. Do you own a camera? Do you take pictures? When, why? What are the occasions? What happens once the film is finished? What do you do with it? Have you ever developed a film yourself or seen someone else do it? Do you know how this is done? What do you know about this process? What are the steps?

2. Do you like to go to the movies or rent them? Which ones are your favourites, and why? Do you know how movies are made? What is the process involved before we can see a movie in theatres? There are three stages in the production of a movie: (1) pre-production; (2) production; and (3) post-production. Which steps are taken during these stages?

3. Are you interested in space research? Do you think that space exploration is essential to the progress of humankind? What can we gain from these explorations? How are they conducted? Do you ever watch when spacecraft are launched? What steps or procedures must be followed for a successful launch? Offer your educated guesses and ask other members of your group for their opinions.

4. What is your field of study? Think of an aspect in your field where you need to explain the process of how to do or make something, or describe something that happened or happens. Explain it to the other members of the group and encourage them to ask questions if they don't understand your explanation.

## Choose a Topic

1. Describe how a photograph is made.

2. Describe how a movie is made.

3. Describe how a spacecraft is launched.

4. Describe any process in your field of study.

# Start the Writing Process

**Brainstorming.** Now that you've selected your topic, brainstorm as many ideas as possible, including examples.

**Selection.** Go over your notes very carefully. Make sure that you select three main ideas that you can develop effectively with appropriate support.

**Development.** Develop the ideas that you have selected. Provide explanations that best illustrate your ideas.

**Organization.** Use the outline form provided to organize the ideas for your essay. Refer to the sample outline to help you.

---

# My Process Essay

Title: _____

Introduction/Hook:

_____

_____

_____

Thesis Statement:

_____

_____

_____

A. Paragraph 1 Topic Sentence:

_____

_____

Supporting Statements and Examples:

_____

_____

_____

B. Paragraph 2 Topic Sentence:

_____

_____

Supporting Statements and Examples:

_____

_____

_____

C. Paragraph 3 Topic Sentence:

_____

_____

Supporting Statements and Examples:

_____

_____

_____

Conclusion:

_____

_____

_____

**Peer Checking.** In pairs, show your outlines to each other. Discuss aspects of the outline that are appropriate and make comments and suggestions about those parts that are unclear, incomplete, or inappropriate.

When evaluating your partner's outline, make sure that

- there are three main ideas;
- each main idea is appropriately developed and clearly supported by illustrations or examples;
- there is a general balance to the discussion of each main idea.

**Revision.** Take note of the comments and suggestions made by your partner and use these to revise your outline.

# Grammar Highlights Box

**The Passive Voice**

In response, the first primary activity *is set* in motion.

Once a body of data *has been accumulated* from reliable observation, the next task is to attempt to make some sense and order out of the data.

To simplify and make sense of these rules a scientist *is urged* to discover an underlying principle.

**Imperative**

Read all directions carefully.

Draw a data table.

Put on your safety goggles.

Examine the rock samples.

**Present Perfect Simple**

Human beings are curious by nature, and it is this very curiosity that *has led* to much that is admirable in what humankind *has produced*.

**Simple Present**

The cycle of scientific development *starts* with an idea, a problem, or a speculation.

A simple set of binoculars drastically *amplifies* our ability to identify a bird in the woods.

**Gerunds and Infinitives**

The methods include *cataloguing* samples, *making* diagrams, *creating* graphs, *using* statistical analysis, and other powerful mathematical tools.

**Compound and Complex Sentences**

Those creatures *who find everyday experience a muddled jumble of events with no predictability, no regularity,* are in grave peril.

However, it is not enough to have powerful instruments *since scientific observation requires both skill and discipline*.

## Task 1: Practising Grammatical Structures

Go back to the sample essay and identify other sentences that contain the grammatical structures illustrated in the Grammar Highlights Box.

## Task 2: First Draft

Use the revised outline to write the first draft of your essay.

- Concentrate on the content, organization, and development of ideas.
- Make sure your introduction includes an interesting hook and a parallel thesis statement.
- Your conclusion must summarize your major points.

## Task 3: Second Draft

Read your draft carefully and check for

- choice of vocabulary
- appropriate transition words
- correct grammar
- punctuation
- spelling

## Task 4: Peer Evaluation

Work in pairs. Exchange your essay and complete the Peer Evaluation Form. Then look at your partner's comments about your essay and make the changes you think are necessary.

---

# Peer Evaluation Form

**Writer's Name:**

**Evaluator:**

| | Yes | No | If not, please comment |
|---|---|---|---|
| ORGANIZATION | | | |
| 1. The introduction grabs my attention. | | | |
| 2. The thesis statement | | | |
| is clear | | | |
| includes three parallel ideas | | | |
| 3. Each paragraph contains | | | |
| a clear topic sentence | | | |

| | Yes | No | If not, please comment |
|---|---|---|---|
| supporting sentences | | | |
| details | | | |
| appropriate transitions | | | |
| CONTENT | | | |
| 1. The choice of ideas is | | | |
| interesting | | | |
| appropriate | | | |
| clearly stated | | | |
| convincing | | | |
| well illustrated | | | |
| GRAMMAR AND MECHANICS | | | |
| 1. Circle or underline any mistakes that you notice in | | | |
| spelling | | | |
| punctuation | | | |
| grammar | | | |

## Task 5: Final Version

1. Write the final version of your essay.

2. Use the Peer Evaluation Form to double-check your work for weaknesses or errors.

3. Proofread your essay before you hand it in.

# EDIT

## Editing 1

There have been 14 errors introduced into the following text. Edit for errors in

- verb form
- subject-verb agreement
- number
- verb tense
- word choice/wrong word
- word form

Global navigation in the 15th century revived interest in the stars and planets. Little change had been made to the model of the universe developed by Ptolemy in second-century Roman times. In this theory, the earth was at the centre of the universe and at rest with no rotation. The sun, moon and planets revolve around this fixed earth. Nicholas Copernicus revived an old idea that was falling by the wayside. He proposed that the earth was not the centre of the universe but the sun and the planets including the earth rotated around it. Copernicus's suggestion was convinced and encouraged a new way of thought at a time when society was opening up to new ideas and technology was evolving to allow new observations. Based on Copernicus' idea, the Danish astronomer Tycho Brahe gathered new, precise information about planet through meticulous observations of the heavens that were 100 time more accurate than previous observations. Meanwhile, make use of the newly developed optical lenses to make a telescope, Galileo extended the process of observation into new domains. On the basis of this observations, Johann Kepler, a German mathematician and astronomy, applied his analytical skills and developed three laws of planetary motion. However, his laws do not explain why they worked. The explanation came from the leap make by Isaac Newton who formulated the law of universal gravitation, this is, all objects in the universe attract each other. The force increases with the

product of their masses and decrease with their distance apart. Kepler's laws

could then be deduced as a consequence of universal gravitation rather than

as a separate set of rules for our planetary systems.

From W. Hanna and C. Cockerton, *The Human Project*, (Scarborough, ON, 1996), 209–11, adapted with permission of Prentice Hall.

# Editing 2

Some errors have been introduced into the following text. Edit it for errors in

- number
- verb form
- word form
- verb tense

When Alexander Graham Bell invented the telephone in 1874, people were

amazed that they suddenly had the ability to talk to other people who were far

away, far beyond the reach of the speaker's unassisting voice. No doubt,

people are just as astounded when the first airplane lifted off the ground in

1903 or when the first television signal was broadcasted in 1939.

Is today's new information technology once again restructuring reality?

Absolutely. We can cite at least three reasons why. First, computers and other

information technology had already altered the world's economy: the produc-

tion of material goods is steadily been replaced by the creation of ideas and

images. Second, new information technology is eroded the importance of

place in our lives. Bell's telephone was able to "reshape people"; however,

because sound travelled along wires, Bell knew exactly where the call is

going. Today, on the other hand, cellular technology allows a person key in a

number and reach another person who could be anywhere on the continent, moving in a car, or flying fifteen kilometres high. Third, there is no more basic foundation of our sense of real. Because of digital imagery it is possible for photographer to combine and manipulate pictures to show anything. For instance, computer animation enables movie producers to have human interact with lifelike dinosaurs. Finally, it is worth considering how new information technology is already reshaping the university and college scene. Books, for example are been replaced by images on tape, film, and computer disk. Textbooks themselves will also be gradually replaced by CD-ROMs. In a world of interactive computer-base instruction, will students still need to travel to classrooms to learn? Will the university or college campus become obsolete?

From J. Macionis et al., *Sociology*, (Scarborough, ON. 1997), p 165, adapted with permission of Prentice Hall Allyn & Bacon Canada.

# EXTEND YOURSELF

## Task 1: Writing a Process Essay or Report

Choose one of the following assignments and write a process report.

1. You are on vacation visiting the ocean. You go for a walk along the beach, and you notice that the water level is very low. In the afternoon, however, the level is much higher. You decide to collect evidence of the sea level for four days, three times a day. Use the steps in the scientific method to report your results.

2. You are a computer expert and your friend is asking you to help buy a good computer. Do some research before you go shopping with your friend.

3. You notice that the street you live on is very noisy at certain times of the day. Use the scientific method to prove your findings.

4. Help your classmates build a model plane, boat, submarine, etc.

### Task 2: Sharing the Story

Bring your report to class and share it in a group. As a group, decide which report is most clearly explained and presented. Share that report with the rest of the class.

# KEEP A JOURNAL

## React to Issues

1. Describe how milk is produced.

2. Describe how a war or any other conflict started.

3. Describe how natural disasters occur.

4. Write about any other issue related to the topic **Science and Technology.**

# GO BEYOND THE UNIT THEME

## Improve Your Writing Skills Even More

Now you have an opportunity to practise writing about other topics not related to the topic **Science and Technology.** However, it is a good idea to use the same writing pattern you have learned in this unit.

Write a process essay on one of the following topics:

- how to pass the English course
- how to study for a test/How to write an essay
- how to be a successful student
- how to find a job
- a topic of your or your teacher's choice

# Unit 8

# The Media

**After completing this unit you will be able to**

- analyze an argumentative essay;

- state your opinion and support it with appropriate evidence, facts, and examples;

- write argumentative essays.

# GET READY

## Task 1: Let's Talk About the Media

Work in a group and discuss at least five of the following questions. Record your answers and report the information to the rest of the class.

1. List the mass media in order of importance (TV, radio, movies, print, etc.) and explain why you rank ordered them in such a way.

2. How many hours a day do you spend reading the paper, listening to the radio, watching TV, or surfing the Internet? When, during the day, do you spend time doing these things? What is so special about the time of the day you spend reading the paper, watching TV, etc.?

3. Can you recall the first time you started reading newspapers on a regular basis? Do you remember why you started? What kinds of articles do you read in a newspaper? Which section(s) do you always read in detail and why? Which ones do you skip, and why? If you don't like reading daily papers or magazines and periodicals, what are your reasons?

4. What kinds of programs do you listen to on the radio? Which radio stations do you listen to, and why?

5. What about TV programs? List the kinds of programs you watch on TV. Describe them briefly and state why they are your favourites. Which programs don't you ever watch and what are your reasons for avoiding them?

6. How comfortable are you with the Internet? Do you have your own computer or do you depend on the one in your school? What kinds of information are you looking for on the Internet that you won't find on TV, the radio, or in the paper?

7. Do you think that we are bombarded with too much information so that we often cannot "see" clearly or judge for ourselves what the real issues are, or are we still able to maintain our views and not be influenced by the media?

8. In your opinion, what is the role of media in general? Are we getting the "right" objective information? Can we be influenced by the kind of information, and the way it is presented to us? What is the power of media on us as individuals? Discuss some important aspects of power and its effects on us.

9. Do you ever "take a break" from the media? If you do, when do you take that break? If you don't, would you consider it, and why or why not?

## Task 2: Let's Freewrite

Take 15 minutes to write about one of the issues discussed in your group that interests you. Then, with a partner, read each other's work and discuss why you decided to react to a specific issue.

# ANALYZE

## Task 1: Predicting Information

Before you read the following essay, work in groups to answer the questions below.

1. What knowledge do you have about television programs that contain violence, and their effects on children and teenagers? Have you read or heard about this issue before? Share any important information with your group.

2. Do you believe that TV has such power over young people and, if so, why? If you disagree, give your reasons.

3. If you believe that violence on TV affects children and teenagers, what would be some ways of solving this problem? Do you think that children and adolescents in your country are exposed to the same degree of TV violence as the young people in North America? Why or why not?

4. Do you think that there is more violence and crime in North America as a result of more exposure to television violence? Why or why not?

## Task 2: Analyzing the Main Arguments and Supporting Facts

The following essay provides arguments against television programs that contain violent scenes. Read it and respond to the questions below.

## Sample Essay: Television Violence

American and Canadian children and teenagers spend more time watching television than they do engaging in any other activity besides sleeping. According to the Ontario Ministry of Education, Canada, they spend an average of 15,000 hours watching TV as compared with 11,000 hours in school, and according to the American Psychological Association, American children who watch 2 hours of TV per day (well below the national average) will see about 8,000 murders and 100,000 other acts of violence by the time they leave elementary school. These disturbing facts have lead many researchers to study what these young people are watching and what effects these programs have on them. It is a fact that the socialization that occurs during childhood is crucial and that children are particularly vulnerable to the stimuli they receive during this time. Therefore, it is hardly surprising that psychologists, educators, and parents are concerned about television's influence on children's development and have protested against the excessive number of violent scenes shown on television.

This situation has led many researchers to look at the effects of violence on children and teenagers. The results of their studies, mostly conducted in the United States, do not always agree. Some analyses contend that violent scenes on television can induce aggressive behaviour in young viewers. Others claim that it is not possible to conclude that television violence has negative effects on most children though they acknowledge that some children can be influenced. It would appear that the impact of violent television scenes largely depends on the form of violence broadcast. For example, a violent act that is punished will have little or no negative impact. Thus researchers are careful to qualify their statements when describing the effects of television violence on young people.

Subsequent, more in-depth studies conducted by Agee, Ault, and Emery (1989) have shown that the effect of violent television content is more subtle. For example, they observed that violent content has an undeniable impact on young viewers of both sexes, but that these effects are contradictory, sometimes even opposed. Thus, some young viewers adopt aggressive behaviour while others feel victimized and fearful. This observation led the researchers to believe that television violence has profound effects which are manifested in more subtle ways than simply aggressive behaviour. For example, they also observed that children who watch many television programs with a violent content sometimes become desensitized to real violence. In this context, some psychologists have compared the effects of television violence on young viewers with that of smoking on lung cancer. The one is not necessarily the cause of the other, though there is an undeniable link between the two. Perhaps the best evidence for a causal link between television watching and violent behaviour comes from a study that compared rates of violence in three similar towns one of which did not have television (Will, 1993). He claims that two years after television was introduced into that remote community, the rate of physical aggression soared by 45 percent for both boys and girls, while it did not change in the two other towns that already had television.

The most convincing theoretical argument that violent behaviour is linked to television watching is based on social learning theory and Albert Bandura's extensive research that children who see fictional characters on television being rewarded for their violent behaviours will not only learn those behaviours but will also perform them when given the opportunity. Children need not directly participate in a behaviour or be personally rewarded for it in order to learn it. They can learn the behaviour simply by watching someone else do it, and if the model is rewarded, they are more likely to perform that behaviour themselves in the future in similar situations. Furthermore, some sociologists' interpretation of the impact of violence on children is even more complex. They claim that the effect is often manifested in the short run and is not as direct as others have believed it to be. They maintain that children's living conditions combined with the exposure to television violence are a contributing factor in children's behaviour. In other words, when scenes of television violence are received in a poor milieu where people have difficulty feeding, clothing and housing themselves adequately, they can have much more harmful consequences than when they are received in a privileged milieu.

The findings of numerous studies on television violence underline the complexity of this issue. In reality, these contradictory findings simply constitute a good excuse for governments and television producers who wish to ignore the results to continue to include violent content, undeniably for the sake of profit. It is therefore the duty of researchers, educators, and parents to put pressure on their governments and television networks to minimize the production of such programs so that children and adolescents can spend more time on other productive and useful things, and eventually become more productive, responsible, and less violent members of society.

From C. Morris, *Understanding Psychology*, (Upper Saddle River, NJ, 1996), 313–315, adapted with permission of Prentice Hall, and from M. Martin, *Communication and Mass Media*, (Scarborough, ON, 1997), 133–134, adapted with permission of Prentice Hall.

1. After reading the essay, how do you feel about the problem?

2. What is the writer's opinion of the effects TV violence has on young people? Do you agree or disagree with him? Why?

3. According to the writer, why are researchers, educators, and parents concerned about the influence of television on children and teenagers?

4. What specific evidence does the writer provide to show the link between watching violence on television and committing a crime or a violent act? List the specific facts.

5. Does the writer present any other possible explanations for young people's violent behaviour besides the exposure to undesirable television programs? What are they? Can you think of any other causes of violent behaviour?

6. Do all young people "adopt aggressive behaviour," or are there other behavioural patterns that researchers have also observed? What are they?

7. How do the psychologists' and sociologists' views differ in regard to television violence and the effects on children and teenagers?

8. Does the writer offer any solutions to this problem? How specific is he? Provide evidence, and then add your own list of specific solutions.

## Task 3: Providing Sources and Evidence

Read the essay one more time and provide either the sources or their findings in regard to television violence and the effects on young people. The recording of information for some findings is incomplete. Complete the table below.

| Name of Source | Research Study and Its Findings |
|---|---|
| Ontario Ministry of Education, Canada | |
| | American children who watch 2 hrs. of TV per day see: 8,000 murders, 10,000 acts of violence by end of elem. school. |
| Mostly the U.S. research studies | 1.<br><br>2. |
| | More subtle effects of violent TV content. *e.g.,* |
| Some psychologists (no specific names provided) | |
| G. Will (1993) | |
| | Children are more likely to perform the behaviour they observed themselves in similar situations. |
| Some sociologists' findings (no specific names provided) | |

## Task 4: Making Opposing Arguments

Take five to ten minutes to make a list of opposing statements in regard to television violence and its effects on young people. Then sit in a group and share your ideas. Make sure that you provide evidence for your statements whenever possible.

For example: If the argument is true that TV violence promotes criminal behaviour in young people, then all of us may be criminals or commit a violent act at one point. However, this is not true. Most people are good, honest, and law-abiding citizens.

# LEARN TO WRITE EFFECTIVELY

## An Argumentative Essay

The essay you just read is an example of **argumentation.** Typically in an argumentative essay, the writer chooses to focus on either the positive or negative aspects of an issue or subject. In other words, the topic must be an issue that has two sides. After completing her own research, the writer then decides which side she is going to take.

You use this type of essay to discuss your point of view in regard to an issue that matters to you. Try to convince your reader to accept your opinion by appealing to his reasoning. Your point of view could be either positive or negative, either for or against an issue.

To make sure that your opinion is believable and therefore convincing to the reader, your statements must be provable. That means that you provide facts and evidence from credible sources and authorities to support your argument. For example, you may write

Research shows that some children who are exposed to violent television programs on a regular basis may commit a violent act or crime at some point in the future.

Versus

I believe that children who are exposed to violent television programs on a regular basis will become criminals or will commit a violent act at some point in the future.

The first argument is provable because it is the result of scientific research and the evidence can be found in published material. Also, the fact that the statement is worded cautiously using the word "*some* children" and the modal "*may* commit" indicates that not "*all* children *will* become criminals when exposed to violent television programs." The second statement, however, is based on your personal view, which is highly emotional and subjective or biased. It includes "*all* children who watch violent programs" and contains the modal word "*will* commit," which expresses the strongest degree of certainty. This kind of statement is not provable because it is based on your opinion.

This does not mean that you cannot use examples from your personal experience or someone else's to support your argument. However, use statements that are carefully worded and clear with appropriate information that directly supports your argument.

For instance, if your argument is that "television violence may affect some children and promote violent behaviour," the following example will support that statement.

> When my friend Sammy was young, he and his older brothers used to watch a lot of violent programs on television while their mom was at work. No one was ever home to supervise the kids and they had to learn on their own how to take care of themselves. They used to go into small grocery stores and steal, mostly food. Later, they started robbing those same stores, and they never got caught. Sammy's brothers ended up in jail much later for a serious crime—they tried robbing a bank.

In argumentative writing, however, the best support for your argument comes from factual information—credible sources, statistics, experts, authorities, published material, research studies, scientific evidence, etc. You can either quote the source directly, or you can paraphrase the information. It is important to indicate the source in either case. When you quote or refer to another author or authors, you can use certain expressions or words to indicate this. Look at the list below.

## Direct or Indirect Quotes

According to (author's name), . . .

   Based on (author's, researcher's, association's name) research, findings, . . .

   Studies, research, findings, results, etc. *show/have (has) shown* that . . .

(author's name) *says that* . . .

| | |
|---|---|
| *claims* | *writes* |
| *states* | *maintains* |
| *indicates* | *explains* |
| *confirms* | *contends* |

To make your argumentative essay even more convincing, it is a good idea to present the opposing arguments to the issue. However, when you do that, make sure that you expose weaknesses in these opposing statements. For example, you can write

> If fictional characters on television are rewarded for their violent behaviour, television networks are sending the message that it is acceptable to behave violently.

> If governments and television networks ignore the research findings because they are not conclusive, and continue to produce violent programs on television, our children will undoubtedly be negatively influenced by them.

## Typical Transition Words for Argumentative Essays

Transition words used to persuade your reader depend on which essay pattern(s) you might be using. To prove your point you may use examples, causes and effects, comparison or contrast, etc.

Other types of useful words are those that

| Introduce Generalizations | Provide Evidence | Point out Exceptions |
|---|---|---|
| generally | it is a fact | there are exceptions to the rule |
| typically | there is evidence | an exception to that is |
| as a rule | undeniably | with the exception of |
| most of the time | the best evidence | this does not include |

## Task 1: Identifying Transition Words and Direct or Indirect Quotes

Go back to the sample essay and underline all the transition words and any direct or indirect quotes.

## Task 2: Completing the Sample Outline

Now read the essay more carefully to complete the following sample outline. Compare your finished outline to a partner's outline.

# Sample Outline

**Title:** _____

Introduction/Hook:

_____

_____

_____

Thesis Statement:

_____

_____

_____

A. Paragraph 1 Topic Sentence:

_____

_____

Supporting Statements and Examples:

_____

_____

_____

B. Paragraph 2 Topic Sentence:

_____

_____

Supporting Statements and Examples:

_____

_____

_____

C. Paragraph 3 Topic Sentence:

_____

_____

Supporting Statements and Examples:

_____

_____

_____

Conclusion:

_____

_____

_____

# WRITE

## Brainstorm Together

### Task 1: Agreeing and Disagreeing

First, work on your own. Score from 1 to 4 how strongly you agree or disagree (1 being strongly agree and 4 strongly disagree), with the following statements and jot down some reasons for your decisions. Then, in a group, discuss your answers. Finally, in your group, make a list of additional controversial statements and share them with the rest of the class.

_____  1. The media are objective when informing the general public of current events.

_____  2. In an authoritarian system people have a hard time discovering the truth because the government controls the media.

_____  3. The media have a tremendous influence on children's personality and social development.

_____  4. Violence on TV does not encourage violent behaviour in children and teenagers.

_____  5. We have no control over mass media effects on us.

_____  6. The media make us apathetic.

_____  7. Mass media are informative, educational, and entertaining.

8. Being informed by mass media means that we are more
knowledgeable and, as a result, more involved in social and
political processes.

_____

9. The media have no respect for famous people's private lives. They
have no right to intrude on one's privacy.

_____

10. The media are an important part of our life and we wouldn't be
able to survive without them.

_____

## Task 2: Freewriting

Take 15 minutes to write about one of the issues discussed in your group
that you strongly agreed or disagreed with. Try to think of the reasons and
examples to support your view.

## Task 3: Adding Information

Decide whether your freewriting contains enough information to be your
starting point for one of the topics listed below. If you are not happy with it,
choose another topic and brainstorm new ideas and examples to support
your view. Use the notes you took during the group discussion.

# Choose a Topic

Look at the following list of topics. Select one you would like to write about.
Take a stand (for or against) and write an argumentative essay.

1. In democratic societies mass media are/are not objective when informing
   the general public about current events.

2. The media have a positive/negative influence on children.

3. Mass media are informative, educational, and entertaining.

4. Mass media have the right/have no right to invade famous
   people's privacy.

5. Mass media are/are not a necessary part of our daily lives.

# Start the Writing Process

**Brainstorming.** Now that you've selected your topic, brainstorm as many
ideas as possible, including examples.

**Selection.** Go over your notes very carefully. Select three main ideas that
you can develop effectively with examples.

**Development.** Develop the ideas that you have selected. Provide examples
with supporting statements and details that best illustrate your point of view.

**Organization.** Use the outline form provided to organize the ideas for
your essay. Refer to the sample outline to help you.

# My Argumentative Essay:

**Title:** _____

Introduction/Hook:

_____

_____

_____

Thesis Statement:

_____

_____

_____

A. Paragraph 1 Topic Sentence:

_____

_____

Supporting Statements and Examples:

_____

_____

_____

B. Paragraph 2 Topic Sentence:

_____

_____

Supporting Statements and Examples:

_____

_____

_____

C. Paragraph 3 Topic Sentence:

_____

_____

Supporting Statements and Examples:

_____

_____

_____

Conclusion:

_____

_____

_____

**Peer Checking.** In pairs, show your outlines to each other. Discuss aspects of the outline that are appropriate and make comments and suggestions about those parts that are unclear, incomplete, or inappropriate.

When evaluating your partner's outline, check that

- there are three main ideas;
- each main idea is appropriately developed and clearly supported by examples;
- there is a general balance to the discussion of each main idea.

**Revision.** Take note of the comments and suggestions made by your partner and use these to revise your outline.

# Grammar Highlights Box

The following grammar structures will help you put your ideas together effectively and edit your work.

**Present Perfect Simple**

This situation *has led* many researchers to look at the effects of violence on children and teenagers.

Some psychologists *have compared* the effects of TV violence on young viewers with that of smoking on lung cancer.

**Complex Sentences: Adjective Clauses, Noun Clauses**

American children *who watch 2 hours of TV per day* will see about 8,000 murders while in elementary school.

The rate of physical aggression did not change in the two other towns *that already had television.*

When scenes of television violence are received in a poor milieu *where people have difficulty taking care of themselves adequately,* they can have a much greater impact.

Others claim *that it is not possible to conclude that violent scenes on TV can induce aggressive behaviour in young viewers.*

It would appear *that the impact of violent TV scenes largely depends on the form of violence broadcast.*

This observation led the researchers to believe *that TV violence has profound effects on the young.*

**Compound/Complex Sentences**

*Therefore, it is hardly surprising that psychologists, educators, and parents are concerned about TV's influence on children's development and have protested against the excessive number of violent scenes that are shown on TV.*

*Others claim that it is not possible to conclude that television violence has negative effects on most children though they acknowledge that some children can be influenced.*

## Task 4: Practising Grammatical Structures

Go back to the sample essay and identify other sentences that contain the grammatical structures illustrated in the Grammar Highlights Box.

## Task 5: First Draft

Use your revised outline to write the first draft of your essay.

- Concentrate on the content, organization, and development of ideas.
- Make sure your introduction includes an interesting hook and a parallel thesis statement.
- Your conclusion must summarize your major points.

## Task 6: Second Draft

Read your draft carefully and check for

- choice of vocabulary
- appropriate transition words
- correct grammar

- punctuation
- spelling

## Task 7: Peer Evaluation

Work in pairs. Exchange your essay and complete the Peer Evaluation Form. Then look at your partner's comments about your essay and make the changes to your essay that you think are necessary.

# Peer Evaluation Form

**Writer's Name:**

**Evaluator:**

|  | Yes | No | If not, please comment |
|---|---|---|---|
| ORGANIZATION | | | |
| 1. The introduction grabs my attention. | | | |
| 2. The thesis statement | | | |
| is clear | | | |
| includes three parallel ideas | | | |
| 3. Each paragraph contains | | | |
| a clear topic sentence | | | |
| supporting sentences | | | |
| details | | | |
| appropriate transitions | | | |

|  | Yes | No | If not, please comment |
|---|---|---|---|
| CONTENT | | | |
| 1. The choice of ideas is | | | |
| interesting | | | |
| appropriate | | | |
| clearly stated | | | |
| convincing | | | |
| well illustrated | | | |
| GRAMMAR AND MECHANICS | | | |
| 1. Circle or underline any mistakes that you notice in | | | |
| spelling | | | |
| punctuation | | | |
| grammar | | | |

## Task 8: Final Version

1. Write the final version of your essay.

2. Use the Peer Evaluation Form to double-check your work for weaknesses or errors.

3. Proofread your essay before you hand it in.

# EDIT

........................................................

## Editing 1

There are 16 errors in the following text. Edit for errors in

- articles
- word choice/wrong word
- verb form

I confess, I am a media junkie. I believe that I have reached a breaking point and I need help. Let me tell you how I know this for fact. You know how a chain smoker needs to light up his first cigarette before opening his eyes in the morning. I, on the other hand, reach at my remote control and turn on the TV, only to be greeting by my old friends from the newsrooms or talk show hosts and their guests. As I go through my morning ritual, I "interact" with them by nodding my head in agreement or disapproval. Recently, I caught myself in the bathroom mirror doing this, which I interpreted like the first alarming symptom of my addiction to the media. From that moment, I started paying close attention to my behaviour and recording it, and this is summary of my findings.

Not only do I turn on the TV first thing in the morning, I subscribe to daily paper, which I read while having coffee in the kitchen, and as I get to my car, I turn on the radio to hear the latest news so as not to miss anything of great importance. In my office, a set of different daily papers and magazines already sitting on my desk. However, I don't look at them before I check my email and the Internet. During lunch, the conversation is usually quite heated in regard to the latest political, economic, social, and sports events. Bulk of my work is done in the afternoon. By six, I am already in my car with the radio on. As I enter my apartment, the first thing I do is turn off the TV. Missing important in-formation, a good show, or a movie must be a disaster. By midnight, I am completely exhausted and my head is spinning. I make sure that all the phones in the house are disconnected, all the gadgets are turned off, and the blinds are tightly closed so that I can to sleep in total peace and darkness for seven hours before the next day's media fix.

I finally made firm decision that I would no longer live for the media. The only way to save myself from this madness is to start fasting. That means no radio, no television, no print, no Internet for at least month. To help myself survive through the first tough period, I am going on a two-week vacation to China, and I don't speak a word of Chinese. This should help somewhat. In meantime, I'll pick up a few good books I've been wanting to read for some time and some new CDs of my favourite music. By the period I come back, I hope to be at least half-cured, and ready to click on or read about only what interests me. I truly hope it works!

# Editing 2

Errors have been introduced into the following text. Edit it for errors in

- subject/verb agreement
- number

- verb tense
- word form

Although not all sociologists agree, the media can be considered an emerging social institution. Furthermore, there is considerably disagreement concerning the media's exact influences on our lives, but the fact is that few parts of our lives remain untouched by them. Far beyond serving simply as source of information, the media also influences our attitudes toward social issues and other people, and even our self-concept. Because the media are such significant shapers of public opinion, all totalitarian governments attempt to maintain tight control over them.

The media is a relatively recent historical development, owing their origins to the invention of the printed press in the 1400s. This invention has had immediate and profound consequences on virtually all other social institutions, the family and religion, legal, political, economic, science, and military institutions. The printing of the Bible altered religion, for instance, while the publication of newspapers dramatically altered politics. From these beginnings, a series of inventions—from radio and movies to television and, more recently, the microchip—made the media an increasingly powerful force.

Indeed, one of the most significant question we can ask about this new social institution is, Who controls it? That control, which in totalitarian countries is obvious, is much less visible in democratic nation. However, we might conclude that the media in a democratic nation represent the varied interests of the many groups that made up that nation. Or, that the media—at least a country's most influential newspapers and television stations—represent the interests of the political elite, the wealth and powerful who use the media to mold public opinions.

Since the media are so influential, the answer to this question of control are of more than passing interest, and further sociological research on it can contribute to our better understanding of contemporary society.

From J. Henslin and A. Nelson, Sociology, (Scarborough, ON, 1996), 97, 99, adapted with permission of Prentice Hall.

# EXTEND YOURSELF

## Choose a Topic

Choose one of the following tasks to write an argumentative essay:

1. Follow a top story in daily papers, on TV, and on the radio for three days. Take notes over this period of time. Date the information and record which newspaper you read, and the radio station and TV channel you listened to. Get the information from a variety of media so that you can get a more realistic picture of the current event. Go over all your notes and react to the factual information by taking a stand. In your essay, discuss whether you think the story was presented objectively or

not. Support your argument with the factual information from your notes to defend your point of view.

With your essay, submit all the sources of information that you used in order to write your essay.

2. Watch some of your favourite programs on TV (comedies, movies, documentaries, news programs, game shows, or any others). Choose one category and write a persuasive essay stating why we should watch those programs.

3. Choose a movie to persuade your reader to go see it. Be convincing by stating clear reasons why this movie is worth seeing.

4. Go to a public library and browse through some of the most popular national newspapers and magazines (the *National Enquirer*, *People*, etc.) and write an argumentative essay why people should/should not read such papers. Provide evidence using examples to support your point of view.

# KEEP A JOURNAL

## React to Issues

Something to write about

1. TV programs I hate

2. We must all read daily papers on a regular basis

3. We can shop without being bombarded by advertisements and TV commercials

4. Any other issue related to **The Media**

# GO BEYOND THE UNIT THEME

## Improve Your Writing Skills Even More

Now you have an opportunity to practise writing about other topics not related to the topic **The Media**. However, it is a good idea to use the same writing pattern you have learned in this unit.

Write an argumentative essay on one of the following topics:

- write a letter to a newspaper editor about an issue that concerns you
- no more capital punishment
- stop destroying our environment!
- a topic of your or your teacher's choice

# Appendix

From M. Frank, Modern English, (Englewood Cliffs, NJ, 1993), adapted with permission of Regents/Prentice Hall.

# VOCABULARY DEVELOPMENT: FORMING AND RECOGNIZING NOUNS

**Note:** Only nouns, verbs, adjectives, and adverbs have derivational forms. Derivational forms consist chiefly of special endings that may

| | |
|---|---|
| change one part of speech to another | engage + ment = engagement<br>destroy + tion = destruction<br><br>nation + al + ize + ation = nationalization |
| distinguish one part of speech from another | distance = noun<br>distant = adjective |

The derivational forms of nouns consist of the following suffixes:

| Function | Suffixes | Examples |
|---|---|---|
| Suffixes changing verbs to nouns:<br>a. suffixes indicating the state of _____-ing | -age, -al, -ance, - ence,<br>- ancy, -ency, -(e)ry, -ment,<br>-t, -tion, -sion, -ure | marriage, arrival, allowance, persistence, consistence, permanency, bribery, arrangement, weight, deviation, invasion, enclosure |
| b. agent suffixes indicating person who _____-s, or a person who is active in _____, or a person who comes from _____ | -ant or -ent, -er or -or or -eer, -(i)an or -arian, -ist | defendant, superintendent, a attendant, manager, governor, auctioneer, New Yorker, Bostonian, librarian, typist |
| c. the suffix that often refers to fields of endeavour, or recreational activities<br>(i) also used as adjuncts in compounds | -ing | fishing, mining, dancing, engineering<br><br>swimming pool, ironing board |

| (ii) they may take adjective modification (iii) they may be used in the plural | | a good cleaning, excellent hunting blessings, weddings |
|---|---|---|
| Endings distinguishing nouns from verbs | | Verb        Noun<br>believe     belief<br>prove       proof<br>live        life<br>defend      defence<br>receive     receipt<br>descend     descent<br>advise      advice |

| Function | Suffixes | Examples |
|---|---|---|
| Suffixes changing adjectives to nouns to indicate the state of being _____ | **-ity, -ness, -th** | activity, sterility, happiness, usefulness, warmth, strength |
| Suffixes distinguishing nouns from adjectives | **-ant** or **-ent** adjective; **-ance** or **-ence** noun | Adjective      Noun<br>intelligent    intelligence<br>distant        distance<br>brilliant      brilliance<br>radiant        radiance |
| Suffixes changing concrete nouns to abstract nouns, to indicate the state of being a _____ | **-hood, -ism, -ship** | brotherhood, childhood, heroism, despotism, fellowship, statesmanship |
| Suffixes changing nouns to other nouns, to indicate:<br>(i)  a doctrine, theory, or school of belief<br>(ii)  a follower or advocate of such a doctrine, theory, or school of belief | **-ism**<br><br>**-ist** | capitalism/capitalist communism/communist impressionism/impressionist terrorism/terrorist |

| | | |
|---|---|---|
| In a few cases these suffixes are added to adjectives rather than nouns | | realism/realist<br>idealism/idealist<br>socialism/socialist |
| Sometimes what precedes these suffixes is not a full word | | pessimism/pessimist<br>baptism/Baptist<br>chauvinism/chauvinist |
| The suffix to distinguish a female person from a male person | **-ess** | waiter/waitress<br>actor/actress<br>host/hostess<br>steward/stewardess |
| Other suffixes denoting a female person | **-ine, -ix, -ette** | hero/heroine<br>aviator/aviatrix<br>suffragist/suffragette |

**Note:** A very large group of nouns have the same forms as verbs.
(e.g.,  answer, control, cough, dance, defeat, dust, exchange, favour, fight, honour, influence, load, mistake, outline, profit, quarrel, request, etc.)

In some cases nouns have the same forms as verbs, but their pronunciation differs.
(e.g.  the ínsult/to insúlt, the óbject/to objéct, the prógress/to progréss)

# VOCABULARY DEVELOPMENT: FORMING AND RECOGNIZING VERBS

The derivational forms of verbs consist of the following suffixes:

| Function | Affixes | | Examples | |
|---|---|---|---|---|
| | Suffixes | Prefixes | Suffixes | Prefixes |
| Added to Nouns = to cause a state of to cause to be a | -ify -ize -en -ate | en- be- ac- im- | beautify solidify memorize apologize frighten lengthen salivate activate | endanger enjoy befriend bewitch acknowledge imprison |
| Added to Adjectives = to cause to become | -en -ize -ate -ify | en- be- | brighten equalize invalidate simplify | enlarge befoul |

Certain roots, although they are not derivational suffixes, always appear in final position with verbs and help identify verbs.

| Verb Roots | Examples |
|---|---|
| -duce | produce reduce |
| -ceive | receive perceive |
| -mit | permit admit |
| -tend | extend intend |
| -sist | persist resist |

# Pronunciation Notes

**Note:** A number of two-syllable verbs differ from the nouns of the same form only in the position of the accent, the nouns being stressed on the first syllable and the verbs on the second syllable.

| Noun | Verb |
|------|------|
| the ínsult | to insúlt |
| the óbject | to objéct |
| the prógress | to progréss |

**Note:** Sometimes the distinction between a noun and verb is a difference in the voicing of the final consonant, with possibly a slight change in the spelling.

| Noun<br>Final Voiceless | Verb<br>Final Voiced |
|------|------|

1. change represented in the pronunciation and spelling

| | |
|------|------|
| the advice/[s] | to advise/[z] |
| the device/[s] | to devise/[z] |
| the bath/[ø] | to bathe/[ð] |
| the breath/[ø] | to breathe/[ð̆] |

2. change represented in the pronunciation alone

| | |
|------|------|
| the house/[s] | to house/[z] |
| the use/[s] | to use/[z] |
| the excuse/[s] | to excuse/[z] |

**Note:** Some verbs have the same form as adjectives but are stressed differently.

| Adjective | Verb |
|------|------|
| séparate | to séparàte |
| pérfect | to perféct |

# VOCABULARY DEVELOPMENT: FORMING AND RECOGNIZING ADVERBS

Most adverbs of manner, many sentence adverbs, and some adverbs of frequency and degree are formed by adding the derivational suffix "-ly" to an adjective.

| **Manner Adverbs** | **Other Adverbs** |
|---|---|
| intelligently | allegedly |
| laughingly | frequently |
| cold-bloodedly | extremely |
| | fully |
| | recently |

Adjectives that already end in "-ly" are often used in unchanged form as adverbs.

| **Adverbs of Manner** | **Adverbs of Time** |
|---|---|
| friendly | early |
| leisurely | weekly |
| lively | daily |
| orderly | monthly |

Because of their special meanings, some descriptive adjectives are not used adverbially with "-ly":  inferior, sick, indicative

## Spelling Rules When Adding "ly" to Adjectives

| Rule | Examples | Exceptions (If Any) |
|---|---|---|
| Final "y" preceded by a consonant is changed to "i" | happily, busily, merrily | |
| Some adverbs from one-syllable adjectives ending in "y" may be written with a "y" or "i" | gayly/gaily<br>dryly/drily | coyly |

| | | |
|---|---|---|
| With adjectives ending in "ble," "ple," "tle," "dle," the "le" is dropped before "-ly" | possibly, simply, gently, idly | |
| With adjectives ending in "ic," "-al" is added before "-ly" | basically, hygienically | publicly |
| In the case of adjectives that end in either "ic" or "ical," the "-ly" is added to the "ical" form | geographically, historically | |
| With adjectives ending in silent "e," the "e" must be retained before "-ly" | extremely, entirely, sincerely | truly, duly, wholly |
| With adjectives ending in "l," the "l" must be kept before "-ly" | beautifully, accidentally, totally | In the case of a few one-syllable adjectives that end in a double "l," one "l" is dropped before "-ly" e.g., dully, fully, shrilly |

Other derivational suffixes that distinguish adverbs

"-ward(s)": frontward(s), backward(s), onward(s)
"-wise": lengthwise, otherwise, counterclockwise
"-where": anywhere, nowhere, elsewhere
"-ever": forever, however, whenever
"-place": someplace, anyplace

There is one derivational prefix that signals adverbs and it is attached mostly to nouns

"a-": apart, apiece, aside, along, ahead, aloud

# VOCABULARY DEVELOPMENT: FORMING AND RECOGNIZING ADJECTIVES

Most adjective derivational suffixes have little semantic content; they simply indicate the part of speech. Adjective suffixes are usually added to nouns or verbs.

| Function | Suffixes | Examples |
|---|---|---|
| changing nouns to adjectives | -(i)al | monumental/industrial |
| | -ar | familiar |
| | -ary or -ery | elementary |
| | -ed | talented |
| | -en | rotten/woolen/wooden/ golden/silken |
| | -esque | picturesque |
| | -ful | hopeful/beautiful |
| | -ic(al) | historic(al) |
| | -ish | stylish/babyish |
| | -istic | characteristic |
| | -less | useless/tasteless |
| | -like | lifelike/ladylike |
| | -ly | friendly/daily |
| | -ous | famous/nervous/envious/ victorious |
| | -ward | backward |
| | -wide | world-wide/country-wide |
| | -y | windy |
| | -th | fifth/ninth/twelfth |
| changing verbs to adjectives | -able or -ible | enjoyable/drinkable/ comfortable sensible/edible/incredible/ possible |
| | -ent or -ant | dependent/observant |
| | -ed | frustrated |
| | -ile | hostile |
| | -ing | boring |
| | -ive | attractive |
| | -(at)ory | congratulatory |

Common suffixes denoting proper adjectives (nationality or religion):

| Suffixes | Examples |
|----------|----------|
| -(i)an | Canadian, Parisian, Italian, Christian, Arabian, Indian, Brazilian, German, Cuban |
| -ish | Irish, Polish, Spanish, Scottish |
| -ese | Chinese, Japanese |
| others | Greek, Israeli, French, Dutch |

# Spelling Rules for Adding Adjective-Forming Suffixes

| Rules | Examples | Exceptions (If Any) |
|-------|----------|---------------------|
| Double the final consonant before a vowel (or "y") | regrettable<br>rotten<br>foggy | |
| Change "y" to "i":<br><br>before the consonant<br>before the vowel | beautiful, pitiless, daily<br>envious, industrial, victorious | ladylike, countrywide<br>babyish |

| Final silent "e":<br><br>drop the final silent "e" before a vowel<br>keep the silent "e" before a consonant | nervous, observant, valuable<br>careful, lonely, tasteless | The "e" is retained after "c" and "g" to prevent a change in pronunciation:<br>e.g., noticeable<br>With some one-syllable adjectives ending in "-able," the dictionary also gives spellings with retained "e" as a second choice:<br>e.g., usable/useable, lovable/loveable movable/moveable<br>Drop "e" before "-th":<br>e.g., width, fifth, twelfth, ninth<br>**Note:** awful but awesome |
| --- | --- | --- |

# Skills Index

# Photo Credits

Pg. 1 Dick Hemingway; Pg. 2 (top) Dick Hemingway (bottom) Imperial Oil Limited; Pg. 22 Matthew Christian; Pg. 48 Dick Hemingway; Pg. 67 Dick Hemingway; Pg. 91 UN/DPI Photo by Milton Grant Copyright © United Nations; Pg. 113 Prentice Hall Archives; Pg. 134 NASA; Pg. 155 Al Harvey